How to Use

History Pockets

History Pockets—Moving West features nine adventurous groups of people who took part in the westward movement that forever changed the face of America. An additional pocket introduces the westward movement to students. The engaging activities are stored in labeled pockets and bound into a decorative cover. Students will be proud to see their accumulated projects presented all together. At the end of the book, evaluation sheets have been added for teacher use.

Make a Pocket

1. Use a 12" x 18" (30.5 x 45.5 cm) piece of construction paper for each pocket. Fold up 6" (15 cm) to make a 12" (30.5 cm) square.

2. Staple the right side of each pocket closed.

3. Punch two or three holes in the left side of each pocket.

Assemble the Pocket Book

1. Reproduce the cover illustration on page 3 for each student.

2. Direct students to color and cut out the illustration and glue it onto a 12" (30.5 cm) square of construction paper to make the cover.

3. Punch two or three holes in the left side of the cover.

4. Fasten the cover and the pockets together. You might use string, ribbon, twine, raffia, or binder rings.

Every Pocket Has...

Overview Page
This teacher reference page describes the activities presented in each pocket.

Pocket Label

Fast Facts Bookmark and Pocket Label
Reproduce the page for students. Direct students to color and cut out the pocket label and glue it onto the pocket. Cut out the bookmark and glue it to a 4½" by 12" (11.5 x 30.5 cm) strip of construction paper.

"Fast Facts" Bookmark

About Page
Reproduce the "About..." page. Use this information and the "Fast Facts" bookmark as references for the activities presented in the pocket.

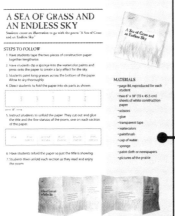

Activities
Have students do the activities and store them in the labeled pocket.

Note: Reproduce this cover for students to color, cut out, and glue to the cover of their Moving West book.

MOVING WEST

NAME: _____

Pocket 1

INTRODUCTION TO
MOVING WEST

FAST FACTS

Moving West . . . . **page 5**
Prepare the bookmark about moving west,
following the directions on page 2. Students
read and share the interesting facts about
the westward movement. Use the Fast Facts
for a quick review during transition times
throughout the day.

ABOUT

Moving West . . . . **page 6**
Reproduce this page for students. Read
and discuss the important information to
remember. Use this page as a reference guide
for the activities in the pocket. Incorporate
library and multimedia resources that are
available.

ACTIVITIES

Map of the Westward Movement . . . . **pages 7 & 8**
The United States government purchased
land or fought over land to increase its size.
Students color in the major land deals of the
1700s and 1800s on the map on page 8 to
see the westward movement process. Then
students answer questions about the map.

**Westward Movement
Time Line** . . . . **pages 9 & 10**
Students are introduced to some important
people and events as they make their own
time line of the westward movement across
America.

Collage of the West . . . . **page 11**
As students learn about the different places
and people along the trails heading west, have
them make a collage of images of the past.

INTRODUCTION TO MOVING WEST

MOVING WEST
FAST FACTS

- America's first pioneers who moved west were fur traders, cattle ranchers, farmers, and miners.

- Almost half a million pioneers traveled through the wilderness on foot, on horseback, and in covered wagons.

- The Wilderness Trail cut through the Appalachian Mountains and helped 200,000 pioneers head west.

- In 1803 President Thomas Jefferson bought land through the Louisiana Purchase, which doubled the size of the United States.

- It took six months for wagon trains to journey to the Pacific Northwest along the Oregon Trail.

- When gold was discovered in 1848, there were 20,000 people living in California. Four years later, 200,000 people made California their home.

- The Homestead Act of 1862 gave any U.S. citizen 160 acres (65 ha) of free land in the Great Plains. Over 600,000 farm families took the government up on this offer.

ABOUT
MOVING WEST

The story of America is a story of movement. Like many Americans today, the Americans of history were often on the move.

Thousands of years ago, the first Americans made the long journey to this land from Europe and Asia. Many generations of these people settled all across the continent, forming a variety of tribal cultures. Today, the descendants of these people are known as Native Americans. For quite a long time, they were the only Americans.

Then, several hundred years ago, visitors began to arrive on America's shores. These were mostly explorers from European countries. They came by ship, sailing in search of riches like gold, silk, and spices. When the explorers went back to Europe, they told stories of a promising new land, rich with resources.

Soon, many people in Europe had the idea of coming to the New World to live. Europe was very crowded. There was not enough land, timber, or food. America seemed to be the answer.

During the 1600s, the British sent many settlers to America. These settlers established colonies along the eastern coast. The thirteen colonies grew quickly from small farming villages into crowded cities. Some people loved the city life. Others longed for open spaces.

To the west lay uncharted miles of forested wilderness and vast tracts of land, just waiting to be tamed. Americans were on the move again, heading west.

The pioneers moved west in three great waves. From the 1770s to the early 1800s, the first pioneers crossed the Appalachian Mountains and settled in the Mississippi and Ohio River valleys. The second great wave took place from the 1840s to the 1860s. Pioneers traveled from the East Coast to the West Coast to settle in Oregon and California. The final movement westward happened in the 1860s, when pioneers settled in the Great Plains. In 1890 the United States government claimed that there were no more frontiers to be settled.

MAP OF THE WESTWARD MOVEMENT

The United States gained new lands during the 1700s and the 1800s. For 100 years, the United States' territory expanded westward. This expansion was a result of exploration, wars with other countries, Indian treaties, and land deals.

Students color the map on page 8 and then answer the questions that follow to learn about the westward movement.

STEPS TO FOLLOW

1. Study the map on page 8. Discuss the different ways the United States obtained the lands west of the thirteen colonies. Use the Fast Facts bookmark for more information.

2. As you talk about the various land deals, have students lightly color the sections different colors.

3. Then have students answer the questions using the information on the map.

4. Share the answers as a class. An answer key is provided for you at the bottom of this page.

MATERIALS

- page 8, reproduced for each student
- pencil
- colored pencils

Answers to questions on page 8.

1. Answers will vary.

2. Mississippi River

3. Gadsden Purchase from Mexico, 1853

4. Great Britain, France, Mexico, and Spain

Name: _____

MAP OF THE WESTWARD MOVEMENT

Directions: Study the map to see how the United States grew during the 1700s and 1800s. Color each section of the map. Then use the map to answer the questions.

1. Original 13 states
2. Area gained by Treaty of Paris, 1783
3. Louisiana Purchase, 1803
4. Ceded by Great Britain, 1818
5. Florida ceded from Spain, 1819
6. Texas, 1845
7. Oregon Country, from Great Britain, 1846
8. Mexican Cession, 1848
9. Gadsden Purchase, from Mexico, 1853

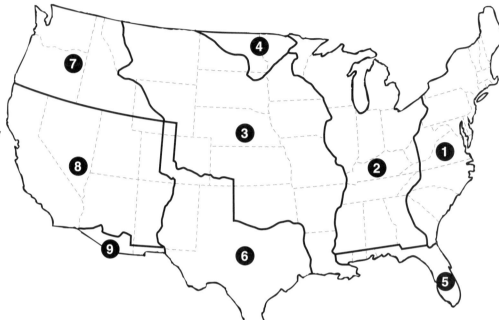

1. Locate your state on the map. In what year did this area of the country become part of the United States?

   _____

   _____

2. What river formed the western border of the United States in 1783?

   _____

3. Which area of the map was the last to come under U.S. control?

   _____

4. According to this map, the U.S. gained land from several different countries. List these countries.

   _____   _____

   _____   _____

   EMC 3704 • Moving West • ©2003 by Evan-Moor Corp.

WESTWARD MOVEMENT TIME LINE

Students put together a time line of special people and events during the westward movement, which lasted from 1775 through 1890.

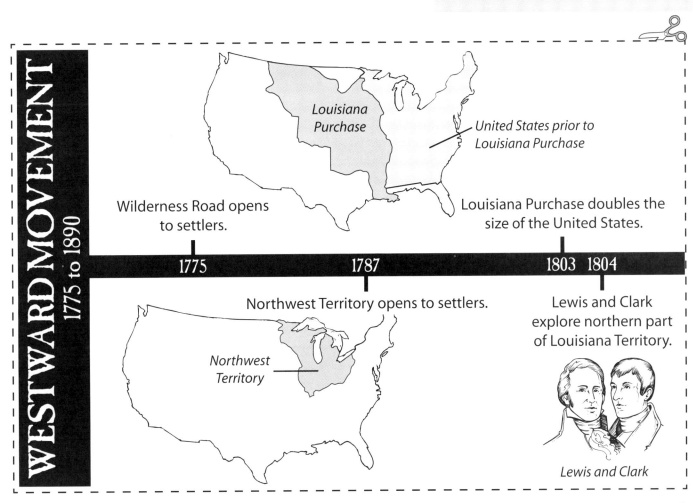

STEPS TO FOLLOW

1. Students cut out the 3 time line sections and glue them together.

2. As a class, read and discuss the dates, people, and events in the history of moving west. Have students color the pictures on the time line.

3. As students read about the important dates, people, and events in each pocket, encourage students to look back at their time lines for reference.

4. Fold the time line and store it in Pocket 1.

MATERIALS

- pages 9 (bottom only) and 10, reproduced for each student
- pencil
- colored pencils
- glue
- scissors

WESTWARD MOVEMENT 1775 to 1890

Wilderness Road opens to settlers.

Louisiana Purchase

United States prior to Louisiana Purchase

Louisiana Purchase doubles the size of the United States.

1775   1787   1803 1804

Northwest Territory opens to settlers.

Northwest Territory

Lewis and Clark explore northern part of Louisiana Territory.

Lewis and Clark

WESTWARD MOVEMENT TIME LINE

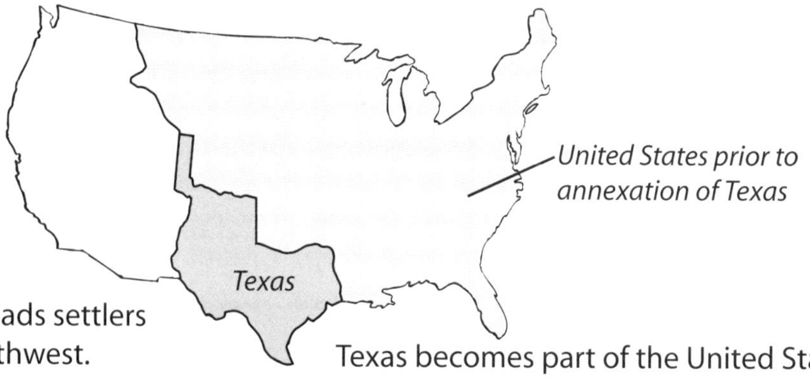

United States prior to annexation of Texas

Texas

Santa Fe Trail leads settlers to the Southwest.

Texas becomes part of the United States.

1821   **1836**   **1845**   **1848**

Missionary settlers arrive in Oregon.

Gold discovered at Sutter's Mill. California Gold Rush begins.

About 3,000 Mormons walk across the Great Plains to join their leaders in Utah.

The country's first transcontinental railroad system is completed.

1856   **1862**   **1869**   **1890**

The Homestead Act gives free land to people who settle in the Great Plains.

The last of the Indian territories opens to settlers. U.S. Census Bureau declares that no frontiers remain.

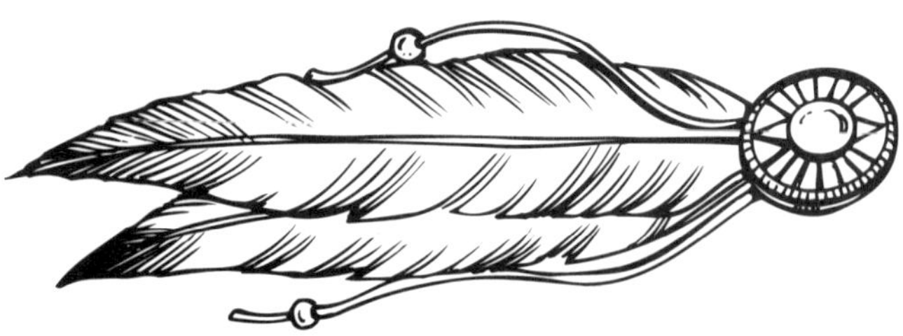

EMC 3704 • Moving West • ©2003 by Evan-Moor Corp.

glue tab

glue tab

COLLAGE OF THE WEST

The westward movement across America was an exciting time in the country's history. The images of the people and places along the way were vivid and colorful. From the pioneers in Kentucky to the railroad builders in California, all contributed to the building of a vast nation.

As an ongoing project, have students add or draw pictures and words to make a collage of the westward movement.

STEPS TO FOLLOW

1. Explain to students that they are going to make a collage of the people and places they learn about as they "travel" west.

2. Have students put the title "Moving West" on a piece of construction paper.

3. After students finish each pocket, brainstorm with them the images and words that come to mind for that pocket. Make a list of the ideas on the chalkboard. For example, Pocket 2 is about early pioneers, so pictures and words could be about Daniel Boone, the Appalachian Mountains, log cabins, the Wilderness Road, furs, and forts.

4. Have students draw or find pictures in magazines of the images discussed and add them to their collages. Encourage students to also add words and phrases to their pictures.

5. Follow this method for all the pockets. After the students have completed the last pocket, they will have collages filled with exciting images of the westward movement.

6. Display the collages in the classroom. Then have students store their collages in Pocket 1.

MATERIALS

- 9" x 12" (23 x 30.5 cm) white construction paper
- pencil
- marking pens
- scissors
- glue
- magazines (old *National Geographic* magazines are ideal)

Pocket 2

THE NEW FRONTIER

FAST FACTS

The New Frontier . . . . **page 13**
Prepare the bookmark about the early pioneers on the frontier, following the directions on page 2. Students read and share the interesting facts about the new frontier. Use the Fast Facts for a quick review during transition times throughout the day.

ABOUT

The New Frontier . . . . **page 14**
Reproduce this page for students. Read and discuss the important information to remember. Use this page as a reference guide for the activities in the pocket. Incorporate library and multimedia resources that are available.

ACTIVITIES

Daniel Boone, Frontiersman . . . . . . **pages 15 & 16**
Students learn about the famous pioneer who helped build the Wilderness Road. They make their own portrait of a frontiersman of Kentucky.

Kitty's Kentucky Diary . . . . **pages 17–19**
A pioneer girl named Kitty wrote all about her first year in Kentucky. Students read her entries and add pictures that describe the monthly activities in Kitty's diary.

George Rogers Clark . . . . **pages 20–22**
George Rogers Clark helped to obtain the Northwest Territory for the United States. Read about this early frontiersman and war hero on page 21. On page 22, have students use a United States map to fill in the current states that make up the Northwest Territory. Students then write a paragraph about which group really "owned" the Northwest Territory: the British, the Native Americans, or the pioneers.

THE NEW FRONTIER

©2003 by Evan-Moor Corp. • EMC 3704

- Pioneers did not have sugar. For sweeteners they used syrup from maple trees, wild honey, or pumpkin juice!

- Pioneer children played with dolls made of rags or cornhusks.

- Pioneers made some of their hard work into play. They would gather with their neighbors to husk corn, make quilts, or build cabins.

- When pioneer children went to school, they studied reading, spelling, and simple arithmetic.

- Many pioneers wore coonskin caps, but Daniel Boone favored a black felt hat.

- Native Americans captured Daniel Boone several times. Once, he stayed with them for almost two years before escaping. Chief Blackfish adopted him into the Shawnee tribe.

- Daniel Boone was asked if he had ever been lost. He replied, "No, can't say as ever I was lost. But I was bewildered once for three days."

- By 1800, 200,000 pioneers had taken the Wilderness Road west.

- George Rogers Clark was a Revolutionary War hero as well as a famous frontiersman.

- The brother of George Rogers Clark, William, was one of the explorers in the Lewis and Clark Expedition.

ABOUT
THE NEW FRONTIER

As the population in the colonies grew, many people became restless. Settlements had sprouted up all along the eastern seaboard. Towns large and small grew up along the many rivers and seaports. Neat farms replaced wild tangles of forest all the way to the Appalachian Mountains.

Across those mountains, the land was claimed by Great Britain. However, the pioneers were not very concerned about borders. They knew that rich, beautiful land lay across the mountains, and they set out to claim the new frontier.

In 1772 a group led by John Sevier traveled into what is now Tennessee and established new communities. Daniel Boone opened the way to Kentucky and brought many families there to live. George Rogers Clark drove the British out of their strongholds to the north. As a result, settlers flooded into the Northwest Territory, an area that now includes such states as Ohio, Indiana, and Wisconsin.

The people who pushed across the mountains to make their homes in the wilderness were very brave. They had to depend upon themselves for everything. They built their homes from logs cut by hand. They made their own furniture and clothing. They had to hunt, gather, or grow their own food.

There were many dangers in the wilderness. The Native Americans were angry with these new settlers on their lands. To make matters worse, the British often paid the Native Americans to attack the settlers and drive them out. Winter weather was harsh, and food was sometimes scarce. Without hospitals or modern medicine, disease and accidents claimed many lives.

The difficulties did not discourage these hardy pioneers. They were confident in their ability to care for themselves. They loved the freedom of working their own land. They worked hard, but they worked for themselves. They felt independent and proud.

No matter how hard the work or how great the danger, these pioneers were determined to seek new homes on the frontier. In the late 1700s, they began to cross the mountains. The trickle of settlers soon grew to a steady stream and at last became a mighty flood.

EMC 3704 • Moving West • ©2003 by Evan-Moor Corp

DANIEL BOONE, FRONTIERSMAN

Daniel Boone was a famous frontiersman who blazed a trail called the Wilderness Road. Students read about this legendary hero and then make a portrait of a frontiersman.

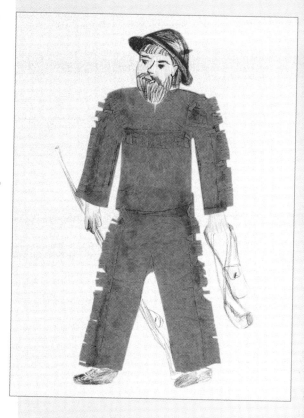

STEPS TO FOLLOW

1. Read and discuss the information about Daniel Boone on page 16. Show students pictures of frontiersmen and the way they dressed.

2. On construction paper or an old file folder, direct students to draw an outline of a large man standing tall.

3. Have students cut out a long-sleeved shirt and a pair of pants from the brown paper. Instruct them to glue the shirt and pants to the man.

4. Then have students cut strips of fringe from brown paper and glue them onto the pants and shirt.

5. Direct them to draw moccasins or cut them out of brown paper.

6. Students draw a "felt" hat to complete the portrait of a frontiersman. Remind students that Daniel Boone preferred a felt hat to a fur one.

7. Have students staple the information about Daniel Boone to the back of the picture.

MATERIALS

- page 16, reproduced for each student
- 9" x 12" (23 x 30.5 cm) tan construction paper or old file folder
- brown paper (grocery bag) crumpled and flattened several times to soften
- pencil
- crayons
- glue
- stapler
- scissors
- pictures of frontiersmen
- Optional: black felt

DANIEL BOONE, FRONTIERSMAN

The year was 1769. Daniel Boone was enchanted with the scene that lay before him. In Boone's eyes, Kentucky was a paradise, brimming with all the gifts nature could offer. He was determined to make it his home.

Boone hurried back to his farm in North Carolina along the same path that had brought him to the wilderness. This was an Indian trail known as the Warrior's Path. It was a narrow footpath and the only known route across the mountains.

Boone told his friends and family about the marvelous country called Kentucky. By 1775 Boone had gathered a group of 30 hardy woodsmen. Together, they set out to build a better road across the mountains. Using axes, they widened the Indian trail by chopping down trees and clearing the underbrush.

The work went smoothly until the men were deep into Kentucky. The Native Americans there were not happy to see white people cutting down trees and opening a wide trail. They attacked Boone and his men several times. Some of the men were killed, but none wanted to turn back. They kept going, cutting their way through the forest and clearing the rocky trail that was named the Wilderness Road.

Finally, they arrived on the banks of the Kentucky River. Here they made a fort, which they named Boonesborough. The fort boasted stout cabins surrounded by a tall log enclosure. The men believed that their families would be safe enough inside the strong, thick walls of the fort.

When the work was finished, Boone returned to North Carolina once again. He and his wife, Rebecca, and their children packed a few belongings and set off on the Wilderness Road. Kentucky was open to settlers, and pioneer families began to pour across the mountains to find new homes in the West.

Daniel Boone had "the itching foot" all his life. In other words, he could never settle down in one place for very long. Boone roamed the western plains until he was nearly 80 years old.

"After a long and fatiguing journey through a mountainous wilderness, in a westward direction, on the seventh day of June following we found ourselves on Red River...and from the top of an eminence, saw with pleasure the beautiful level of Kentucky."

—Daniel Boone

EMC 3704 • Moving West • ©2003 by Evan-Moor Corp

KITTY'S KENTUCKY DIARY

Early pioneers traveled over the rough Wilderness Road to start a new life in Kentucky. Students learn about pioneer life when they read a girl's journal, called "Kitty's Kentucky Diary." Kitty tells readers about her family's first year in Kentucky. She forgot to add pictures, so the students will help her out by adding illustrations to the diary.

STEPS TO FOLLOW

1. Have students cut out the 12 diary entries.

2. Direct them to place the pages in order from January to December.

3. Have students fold the three pieces of white paper in half to make six sheets.

4. Instruct students to glue the 12 diary entries to the front and back of the pieces of paper.

5. Direct students to fold the construction paper in half and then place the ordered diary sheets inside to make a booklet.

6. Help students punch two holes on the left side of the booklet and tie yarn through each hole.

7. On the front construction paper cover, have students write the title "Kitty's Kentucky Diary."

8. Have students read the 12 diary entries and think about the activities that Kitty writes about.

9. Then direct students to draw and color pictures of the activities that are described for each month of the year in the diary entries.

10. Have students read the completed diary to partners.

MATERIALS

- pages 18 and 19, reproduced for each student
- three 8½" x 11" (21.5 x 28 cm) sheets of white copy paper
- 9" x 12" (23 x 30.5 cm) construction paper
- scissors
- glue
- stapler
- hole punch
- two 18" (45.5 cm) pieces of yarn
- crayons or marking pens

KITTY'S KENTUCKY DIARY

January

It's snowing! Outside our cabin, the trees all look like they've been dipped in sugar. It's very exciting because this is the first snowfall on our new cabin roof! Our new cabin belongs to Mama and Papa and my brother Jim and me, Kitty. We just arrived here last summer. We used to live in Virginia, but Papa said it was too crowded there and he didn't have room to draw a decent breath. So, here we are in the woods of Kentucky. Today I will help Mama with the spinning, while Jim helps Papa mend our shoes. Everyone wants to stay close to the warm hearth today!

February

The weather has warmed a bit. Grandfather calls it "the thaw." Jim and I are helping with the sugaring. Papa cut some notches in the big maple trees to let the sap run out. He hung buckets on the trees to catch the sap. Jim and I tote the buckets to the iron kettle where Mama cooks the sap into thick sweet syrup.

March

Papa and Jim are out in the woods cutting trees. Papa wants to clear another acre to plant corn. It is hard work, and they will be hungry when they come in. Mama is roasting some bear meat on the fire, and I made some johnnycake all by myself!

April

We have new neighbors! They are my Aunt Rachel and Uncle Henry. They have two little girls who are only a little younger than me. They've been staying with us while their cabin is built. All the men from the settlement are helping. It is fun to watch them roll the logs into place.

May

May is seed-planting time. Papa plows the field with the help of Tucker, our big gray horse. Jim and I follow behind dropping seed corn in the furrows and covering the rows with warm soil. Mama is planting the kitchen garden with beans and squash and pumpkins—and some flowers too. Mama does love her flowers.

June

How do weeds grow so fast? Papa says we are not to let them creep up on us. Every day Jim and I take our hoes and chop all the weeds out of the corn patch. It is hard, hot work. But Mama says if we want johnnycake to eat, we have to get a good crop of corn. It helps to know that when we finish our rows we can go fishing in the creek!

EMC 3704 • Moving West • ©2003 by Evan-Moor Corp.

KITTY'S KENTUCKY DIARY

July

This morning Mama and I took our pails down to the edge of the clearing to pick blackberries. The thorns are fierce, but the berries are worth it. We picked two whole gallons between us. This afternoon, Mama made a pie for supper, and we cooked down the rest to make fruit leather for the winter.

August

These are long, hot days. Each morning we pick vegetables from the garden. This morning we picked squash. We sliced the squash into strips and laid them on the cabin roof to dry. The squash shrivels up into thin dry bits that, believe it or not, will make tasty pies this winter.

September

Papa and Jim are cutting wood for the winter. Papa felled the trees last year and left them to dry. Now he and Jim must chop up the branches and split the big trunks. Mama needs an endless supply of nice dry wood for cooking. As the weather turns cooler, we'll need extra to keep the cabin warm.

October

It's nut-gathering time. All of us go out into the woods together. It's my favorite job of the whole year! Mama and I like hickory nuts best. Papa says he likes black walnuts better. But they are the hardest of all to shell! I fill up my sack until it is almost too heavy for me to carry. Then I scoop up red and golden leaves into a heap and dive right in. I lie back and look up at the bright blue sky. I am very happy.

November

Have you ever made candles? Mama builds a fire in front of the cabin. She fills her iron kettle with tallow and sets it on the blaze. When the tallow is melted, we dip strings, called wicks, into the hot fat. Then we set the wicks aside to cool and harden, and begin again with fresh wicks. Again and again we dip the wicks until nice fat candles form.

December

At last it is Christmas. Our Aunt Rachel and her family will come to visit, and we will have a feast. Papa and Jim had a good hunt, and Mama is making venison roast and a savory squirrel stew. I'm going to make a pudding out of cornmeal and some of the maple sugar Mama saved just for this special day. Then we will play games, and Mama will read to us all. It will be a jolly Christmas here in our Kentucky cabin.

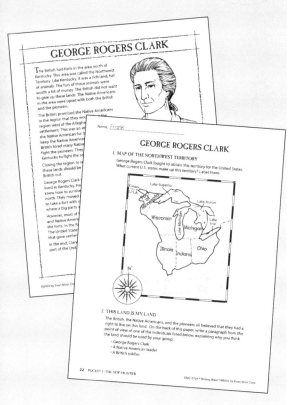

GEORGE ROGERS CLARK

George Rogers Clark was a frontiersman who helped the United States gain more land. This was called the Northwest Territory. The Northwest Territory makes up the current states of Illinois, Indiana, Michigan, Ohio, Wisconsin, and part of Minnesota.

Students read about George Rogers Clark's accomplishments. Then they fill in a map of the Northwest Territory with the current states that make it up. On the back of the map, students write a paragraph about obtaining the Northwest Territory.

STEPS TO FOLLOW

1. Read about George Rogers Clark and the Northwest Territory on page 21 and discuss.

2. Have students study the map on page 22 and direct them to fill in the current states that make up the Northwest Territory.

3. On the back of the map, have students write a paragraph about who the Northwest Territory really belonged to: the British, the Native Americans, or the pioneers. Students will choose to write the paragraph from the point of view of George Rogers Clark, a Native American leader, or a British soldier.

4. Share the paragraphs in class. You may want to take an informal survey of how many students thought the land really belonged to the British, the Native Americans, or the pioneers.

MATERIALS

- pages 21 and 22, reproduced for each student
- pencil
- colored pencils

GEORGE ROGERS CLARK

The British had forts in the area north of Kentucky. This area was called the Northwest Territory. Like Kentucky, it was a rich land, full of animals. The furs of these animals were worth a lot of money. The British did not want to give up these lands. The Native Americans in the area were upset with both the British and the pioneers.

The British promised the Native Americans in the region that they would close the region west of the Allegheny Mountains to settlement. This was an attempt to protect the Native American fur trade and land, and to keep the Native Americans on their side. The British hired many Native Americans to help fight the pioneers. They even sent them to Kentucky to fight the settlers there.

Closing the region to settlement angered the frontiersmen. They felt that all of these lands should be part of the United States. They were determined to drive the British out.

George Rogers Clark was chosen to lead an expedition against the British forts. Clark lived in Kentucky. He was strong and adventurous. He dressed in buckskin clothes and knew how to survive in the woods. With a small band of frontiersmen, Clark traveled north. They moved at night and rested during the day. Sometimes they were able to take a fort with very little fighting. One time, Clark and his men walked into a fort where a big party was underway. The British surrendered without firing a shot.

However, most of the time, the fighting was fierce and bloody. Many pioneers, British, and Native Americans were wounded or killed. The British never regained control of the forts. In the Revolutionary War, the Americans obtained the Northwest Territory. The United States government set up a series of treaties with the Native Americans that gave settlers, not Indians, the right to more and more land.

In the end, Clark and his men were successful, and the Northwest Territory became part of the United States.

Name: _____

GEORGE ROGERS CLARK

1. MAP OF THE NORTHWEST TERRITORY

George Rogers Clark fought to obtain this territory for the United States. What current U.S. states make up this territory? Label them.

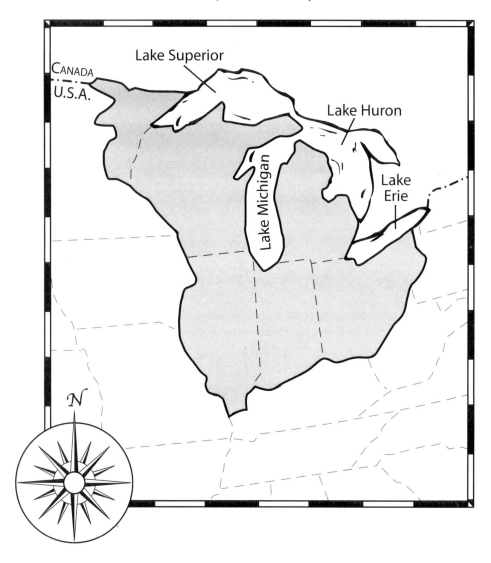

2. THIS LAND IS MY LAND

The British, the Native Americans, and the pioneers all believed that they had a right to live on this land. On the back of this paper, write a paragraph from the point of view of one of the individuals listed below, explaining why you think the land should be used by your group.

- George Rogers Clark
- A Native American leader
- A British soldier

EMC 3704 • Moving West • ©2003 by Evan-Moor Corp

Pocket 3

EXPLORING THE WILDERNESS

FAST FACTS

Prepare the bookmark about explorers and mountain men in the wilderness, following the directions on page 2. Students read and share the interesting facts about exploring the wilderness. Use the Fast Facts for a quick review during transition times throughout the day.

ABOUT

Reproduce this page for students. Read and discuss the important information to remember. Use this page as a reference guide for the activities in the pocket. Incorporate library and multimedia resources that are available.

ACTIVITIES

Students create mobiles of some of the animals described in the journals of Lewis and Clark.

Reproduce these pages for students to make a booklet about three of the mountain men and their fantastic reports from the wilds of the West. Students staple the three stories between two 9" x 12" (23.5 x 30 cm) fringed pieces of brown construction paper. Have students also create cover art for this booklet of amazing stories.

It was hard for people in the East to believe the stories the mountain men told of geysers of hot water or giant bears as big as horses. Students write a riddle about some natural phenomenon that might seem incredible to someone who had never seen or heard of it, and create a pop-up illustration.

EXPLORING THE WILDERNESS

EXPLORING THE WILDERNESS
FAST FACTS

- The mountain men were mostly hunting for beavers. The fur of the beaver was used to make the top hats worn in Europe and in American cities.

- Mountain men often had close encounters with grizzly bears. Hugh Glass was horribly mauled, but survived, and walked out of the wilderness in spite of his injuries.

- Usually mountain men are depicted in books and movies as being loners. Actually, mountain men usually traveled in groups of 40 to 60 men.

- Sacagawea, the Shoshone woman who traveled with Lewis and Clark, made the 2,000-mile (3,219 km) journey while carrying her baby on her back. She was 16 years old.

- Meriwether Lewis took his Newfoundland dog, Seaman, on the expedition.

- In spite of all the dangers and difficulties of the trip, only one member of the Corps of Discovery, Charles Floyd, died on the journey. His death was probably caused by appendicitis.

- After being attacked by Blackfeet Indians, John Colter supposedly walked 200 miles (322 km) back to Fort Raymond with only a blanket on his body for warmth.

- James Bridger's nickname was "Old Gabe." He was only 17 years old when he joined his first expedition.

ABOUT
EXPLORING THE WILDERNESS

In 1801 Thomas Jefferson was elected president of the United States. He had a powerful desire to find out about the mysterious wilderness to the west of the Mississippi. He bought a huge tract of land from France. This was called the Louisiana Purchase.

Explorers

Thomas Jefferson chose his secretary, Meriwether Lewis, to explore the Louisiana Purchase and the lands to the Far West. Lewis asked his friend William Clark to share the job of leading the expedition. Jefferson was interested in finding a water route across the continent.

The two captains gathered 45 men for the trip. They named the group the "Corps of Discovery." One of the men in the group was married to a young Shoshone girl named Sacagawea. Sacagawea helped smooth relations between the expedition and the Native Americans.

Lewis and Clark wrote about the land formations they passed, the appearance of the countryside, and the Native Americans they met. In addition, they sketched and described many new kinds of plants and animals.

During more than two years of travel, the Corps learned that there was no water route across the country. The high Rocky Mountains were a barrier. The amazing discoveries they made softened their disappointment. Their courageous exploration helped to open the West to settlement.

Mountain Men

Strong young men quickly packed a few belongings and headed into the wilderness. They were the mountain men looking for adventure and new riches.

The life of the mountain men was rough. They faced starvation, dehydration, burning heat, freezing cold, animal attacks, and unfriendly Native Americans. In the summer, the men would gather at the summer rendezvous to sell their furs, get supplies, and tell their tall tales of adventure. Many of these mountain men became legends because of their daring feats.

The brave explorers and wild mountain men gave life to some of the most exciting stories in American history.

ANIMALS OF THE WEST

Lewis and Clark recorded in their journals the many different kinds of animals they had never seen back East. They drew prairie dogs, pronghorn antelopes, grizzly bears, and bighorn sheep in their journals.

Students make a mobile with animals "discovered" by Lewis and Clark.

STEPS TO FOLLOW

1. After reading about Lewis and Clark, discuss the different kinds of animals they saw on their expedition.

2. Guide students through these steps to make their mobiles:

   a. Measure, mark, and punch holes in the tagboard as shown.

   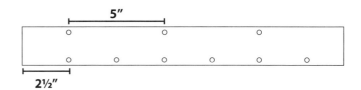

   b. Write "Animals of the West" on the strip.

   c. Staple the strip end-to-end to form a ring. Tie a string to each of the six bottom holes.

   d. Color the four animals from page 27.

   e. Write a short sentence about Lewis and Clark on one rectangle.

   f. Write a short sentence about Sacagawea on the other rectangle.

   g. Cut out the six shapes and glue them to construction paper scraps. Cut around the shapes, leaving a narrow border. Punch a hole in each shape.

   h. Tie the shapes to the strings on the bottom of the strip.

   i. Tie a string from each of the three top holes. Bring the strings together and tie a knot.

3. If desired, have students hang the mobiles around the room. Then the mobile pieces may be placed in a self-locking plastic bag to be stored in the pocket.

MATERIALS

- page 27, reproduced for each student
- 2" x 17" (5 x 43 cm) tagboard
- construction paper scraps
- nine 12" (30.5 cm) pieces of string
- crayons or marking pens
- ruler
- hole punch
- stapler
- scissors
- self-locking plastic bag

ANIMALS OF THE WEST

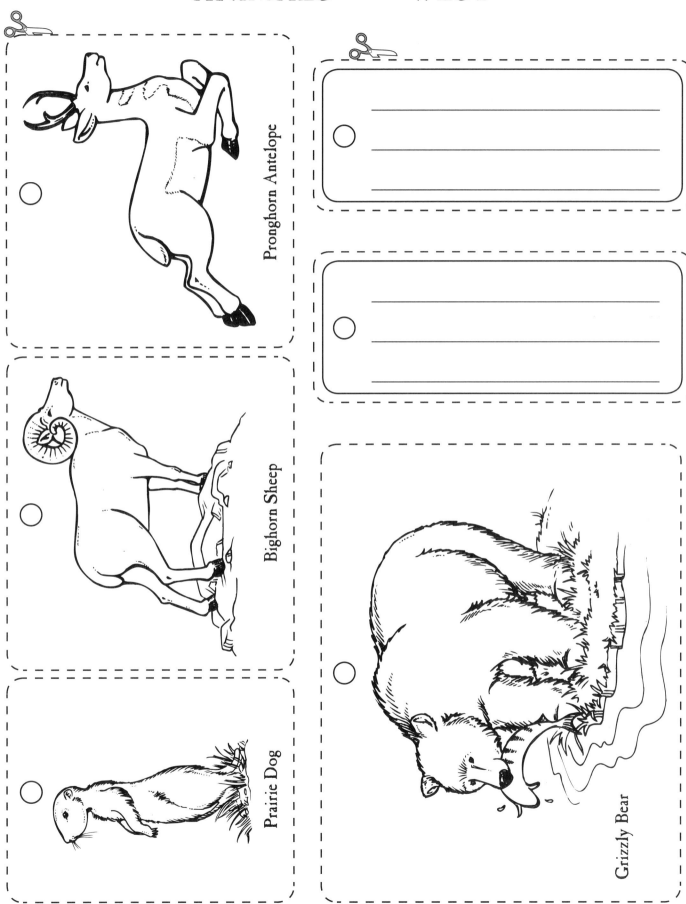

Pronghorn Antelope

Bighorn Sheep

Prairie Dog

Grizzly Bear

John Colter and His Amazing Discovery

John Colter was one of the men who went with Lewis and Clark to explore the West. When it was time to go home, back to "civilization," John Colter decided to stay. He liked the mountains and the wild country. He liked living by his wits, hunting for meat and fur. He did not want to go back to city life.

Therefore, John Colter became one of the "mountain men." These were rough, strong men who did not care for houses and streets. They preferred a house of pine boughs with a roof of stars. They tramped through the woods, living alone and liking it. Sometimes they stayed for a time with friendly Native Americans, and many of them even married Native American women. But they could not stay in one place for long. Adventure was always calling.

Adventure called them into some amazing situations. In the year 1807, John Colter was rambling through the Rocky Mountains hunting beavers. One morning, as he walked along, he heard a strange rumbling sound. Suddenly, only a few yards away, water began to boil and spew up from the earth. In a steamy column it rose, higher and higher, hot droplets raining down around Colter's shoulders. As the geyser subsided, Colter crept closer to examine it. He saw a cone-shaped rock with a deep hole in the center. Gurgling noises still came from the hole, and steam wafted above it.

Startled, Colter backed away from the hole and continued his journey. All through the day, he came upon one odd sight after another. Here was a bubbling puddle of gray and yellow mud. There was a crystal pool of scalding blue water. Every so often, another geyser would spurt up in the distance or nearby. Over all the land, the sulfurous odor of rotten eggs hung in the air.

When Colter next met with his friends, he told them about these wonders. They laughed at his tales of a land where the ground was hot, and boiling water flung itself into the air. Surely, Colter was spinning another of his yarns. The mountain men gave Colter's imaginary landscape a name—"Colter's Hell" they called it.

Of course, today we know that landscape by another name: it's Yellowstone National Park!

The Amazing Story of
Bridger and the Great Salt Lake

Jim Bridger was another of the famous mountain men who wandered the West in search of furs and excitement.

On one of his explorations, Bridger was following the Bear River in Utah to find where it emptied. When the river came to its end, Bridger was standing on a sandy shore looking out at a wide expanse of blue water. Sea gulls circled overhead and a scent of the sea was in the air. He scooped up a handful of water and took a sip.

That quickly, Bridger spat it out again. The water was extremely salty. He was amazed. He decided he had reached the shore of the Pacific Ocean. "This must be an inlet of that ocean. It must reach much farther inland that anyone ever imagined," he thought.

Bridger rushed to tell everyone that he had walked on the shore of the Pacific. They scoffed at his report. This was simply another one of Bridger's tall tales. The Pacific Ocean was hundreds of miles away to the west. What Bridger had found was only a large lake. Everyone knew that lakes were filled with fresh water, not salty water.

Today, we know that the Great Salt Lake is very real indeed. A modern city sits next to its shore, and sea gulls still circle above its salty blue waters.

The Amazing Story of
Moses Harris and the Petrified Prairie

Moses Harris was another mountain man who was famous for his tall tales. Harris was a blacksmith and one of the most experienced guides in the West.

One winter, claimed Harris, he was trapping and hunting in the Black Hills of South Dakota. The snow was deep and the cold was fierce. He and his horse were feeling mighty hungry. Tired and freezing cold, they wandered into a small prairie. Here, to his amazement, the grass was thick and fresh looking. The trees were covered with green leaves. From the branches, birds sang songs of spring.

Taking careful aim, Harris shot at one of the birds, thinking he could cook it for his dinner. When it fell at his feet, it broke into pieces! Harris was astonished to see that the bird was made of stone. He reached down and broke off a blade of grass. It too was brittle and made of stone. He used his pocketknife to chip a piece of bark off one of the trees. Instead of a chunk of wood, he held in his hand a piece of rock.

He slipped that rock into his pocket, and when he returned to "civilization," showed it around to educated folks. They told him that it was indeed a piece of a petrified tree, so part of his story is probably true. As for the petrified grass and the petrified birds—well, what do you think?

SEEING IS BELIEVING

Ask students to think about some of the amazing sights the mountain men found on their travels through the wilderness. Imagine something from nature that might seem puzzling or strange to someone who had never seen it before. A volcanic mountain, a great blue whale, and a saguaro cactus might seem like fantasies if we did not know they were actually real.

Here is an example of a riddle to share with students:

> You can find me in northern California. I am the largest living thing on Earth. I have a wonderful fragrance. There is a national park named for me. When people first heard about me, they thought it was a hoax. They simply could not believe that it was possible for me to be this big. What am I? Answer: Sequoia tree in northern California

After brainstorming a variety of nature's surprises, ask students to choose one and write a riddle about the amazing sight. Students make a pull-through picture frame for their riddle.

STEPS TO FOLLOW

1. Brainstorm a list of natural wonders that are found in the regions west of the Mississippi River.

2. Have students choose a natural wonder and find out facts about the wonder using reference materials that are available.

3. Instruct students to write a riddle about the natural wonder.

4. Then have students cut out the picture frame and glue it to construction paper. Cut around it to make a construction paper border.

5. Have students carefully cut the slits in the picture frame.

6. Direct students to fold the construction paper into thirds. Then have them slip the strip of white construction paper through the cut lines and write the riddle in the first panel. Students pull the strip further and draw a small picture of their natural wonder. In the third section, have students write the answer to the riddle.

MATERIALS

- page 32, reproduced for each student
- 5" x 18" (13 x 45.5 cm) white construction paper
- writing paper
- pencil
- crayons
- scissors
- glue

SEEING IS BELIEVING

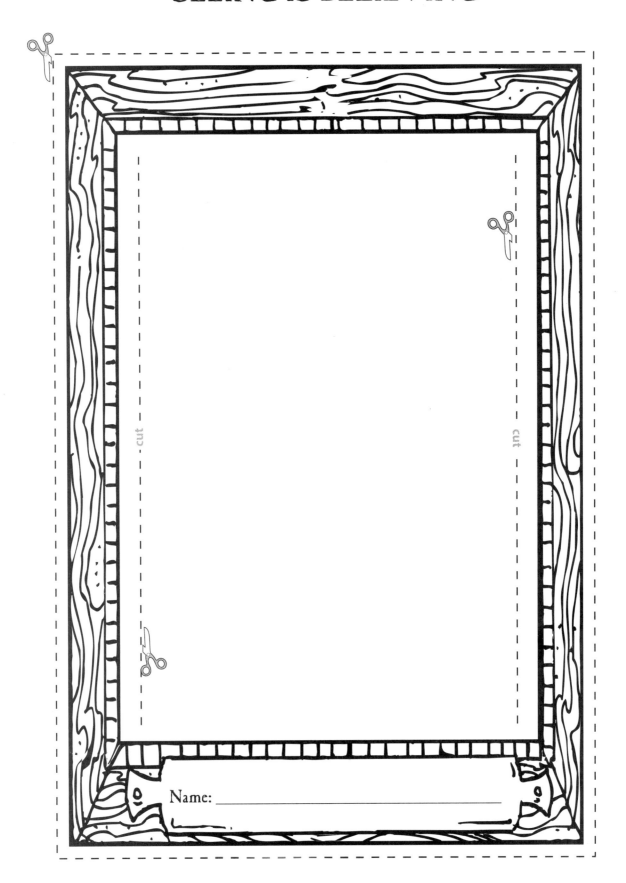

Name: _____

EMC 3704 • Moving West • ©2003 by Evan-Moor Corp.

Pocket 4

MISSIONARIES AT WORK

FAST FACTS

Prepare the bookmark about the missionaries, following the directions on page 2. Students read and share the interesting facts about the missionaries. Use the Fast Facts for a quick review during transition times throughout the day.

ABOUT

Reproduce this page for students. Read and discuss the important information to remember. Use this page as a reference guide for the activities in the pocket. Incorporate library and multimedia resources that are available.

ACTIVITIES

After the students read about Narcissa and Marcus Whitman on page 36, have them answer a letter Narcissa wrote to her brother and sister, asking them to join her at the mission.

The Sager family went west like many others, but they found more than their share of adventure and hardship. Students create a minibook that tells this exciting but tragic story.

MISSIONARIES AT WORK

MISSIONARIES AT WORK

FAST FACTS

- In 1833 an article in a New York Methodist publication stated that Northwest Native Americans were seeking teachers and the white man's "Book of Heaven," the Bible. The mostly fictional article sparked interest in missionary work in Oregon country.

- Missionaries Narcissa Whitman and Eliza Spalding were the first white women to cross the Blue Mountains into Oregon.

- France sent missionaries along with fur traders to Canada and the northern United States.

- Twenty-one Spanish missions were established in California during the 1700s and 1800s.

- Father Jacques Marquette was a French missionary and explorer who traveled down the Mississippi River with his partner, Louis Joliet. After the expedition, Marquette set up a mission among the Illinois Native Americans.

- Father Pierre Jean DeSmet was a Jesuit missionary who established a mission among the Potawatomi in Iowa. In 1840 he set up a mission in the Montana Territory.

- Many new settlements were far away from the missions, so settlers had to rely on traveling preachers called "circuit riders" to perform church services.

ABOUT
MISSIONARIES AT WORK

The settlers who came from Europe to America were mostly believers in the Christian faith. Many of them felt that their faith was the one true way to know God. Some of them believed that it was their job to teach the Native Americans to accept this religion. A few of them devoted their lives to this effort. They became missionaries.

Before the settlers explored the Far West, the French and the Spanish knew the territory well. In the early 1800s, Catholic and Protestant missionaries were sent west.

Missionaries traveled west into the lands where the Native Americans lived. There they built small settlements known as missions. The Spanish established most of the missions in California and the Southwest. The idea of missions had been successful in Spain. The Spanish government and the Catholic Church believed that setting up missions in the Far West would be beneficial. They wanted to convert and educate the native people to their way of life.

Missions usually included farms and schools, as well as churches. The missionaries taught the Native Americans to worship and pray as Christians. They also taught basic skills for living as the settlers lived. These skills included farming, sewing, and sometimes reading and writing.

The Roman Catholic missions grew, prospered, and spread throughout California. Unfortunately, as the missions grew, the Native Americans that worked at the missions did not prosper. This kind of daily schedule was uncomfortable to the Native Americans. They were used to a much freer way of life. Some could not adjust to the structure. They grew depressed and ill, and some died. Others simply ran away. Now and then, angry Native Americans would strike at the missionaries in an effort to regain their old ways of life.

By the 1830s, several missionary organizations became interested in the Pacific Northwest. The Methodist's Mission Society established sites in Oregon. About the same time, the Presbyterian Society of Boston sent more missionaries into southeastern Oregon to work. Later, Roman Catholic missions were established along the lower Columbia River.

Where missionaries went, settlers were soon to follow, changing the Native Americans' world forever.

NARCISSA AND MARCUS WHITMAN

In 1831 four young men from the Nez Perce tribe traveled to St. Louis, Missouri. They said that they wanted to learn the white man's ways and the white man's religion. They asked for missionaries to come to their homes in the territory known as Oregon.

The appearance of Native Americans in a bustling American city caused a sensation. Newspapers printed their story. Church groups around the country began to raise money to send missionaries to travel west to live and teach the Native Americans.

Narcissa and Marcus Whitman were struck with the desire to become missionaries. They were chosen by their church to go and live among the Cayuse Indians. They thought they were doing a good thing to try to change the ways of the Native Americans.

In 1836 the young couple set out for Oregon. They traveled by wagon train with another missionary couple. It was a long, hard journey. At last they arrived at the site they had chosen for the mission. The Cayuse called the place Waiilatpu (Wy-ee-lat-poo), "the place of the rye grass." The Whitmans kept the name for their mission.

Using nothing but hand tools and their own strength, they built a house and some other buildings at Waiilatpu. They plowed the land and planted wheat, potatoes, and corn. They held church services several times each week. Marcus took care of people when they were sick. Narcissa set up a school for the children.

It was a life that was not only difficult for Narcissa, but also very lonely. Above is part of a letter she wrote to her sister, Jane, and brother, Edward, on September 29, 1842.

Now, dear Jane, are you going to come and join me in my labours? Do you think you would be contented to come and spend the remainder of your life on mission ground? It is a dreadful journey to cross the mountains, and becoming more and more dangerous every year... Bring nothing with you but what you need for the way, and a Sunday suit, [and] a Bible... Send the remainder by ship.

I hope [Edward] will come, also, for there will be work enough here to do by that time. At any rate, if you do not come, spend, if you please, all the time you can in writing me....

Affectionately your sister,
Narcissa

Name: _____

Directions: After reading about Narcissa and Marcus Whitman, pretend that you are Narcissa's sister or brother. Answer her letter. Will you choose to go to the mission at Waiilatpu or stay at your home in New York? In your letter, explain the reasons for your decision.

_____
(salutation)

_____

_____

_____

_____

_____

_____

_____

_____

_____

_____

_____
(closing)

_____
(signature)

THE STORY OF THE SAGERS

Students put together a minibook telling the story of the Sager family.

MATERIALS

- pages 38 (bottom only)–41, reproduced for each student
- 4½" x 6" (11 x 15 cm) construction paper
- scissors
- stapler
- pencil
- crayons or colored pencils

STEPS TO FOLLOW

1. Have students cut apart the pages of the minibook and arrange them in the correct order.

2. Direct students to staple the minibook together, using the construction paper as a backing.

3. Read the story of the Sager family as a class, with partners, or independently.

4. Encourage students to draw and color pictures to reflect what is happening in the story.

staple

staple

The Story of the Sagers

staple

staple

In 1844 Henry Sager was a hardworking Missouri farmer. Times had been hard in Missouri. Like other Missouri farmers, Henry Sager heard stories about the Oregon country. He dreamed of a better life for his large family. Many of his neighbors were joining wagon trains. They were bound for the rich new land. Henry decided that his family would go too.

1

THE STORY OF THE SAGERS

Henry and Naomi Sager had six children. The two boys were oldest. John was 13, and Francis was 11. The four girls—Catherine, Elizabeth, Matilda, and Louise—ranged in ages from 9 to 2. Naomi was expecting a baby in a few months. She did not want to make the journey, but Henry was determined. So the family got ready to go.

2

They joined a wagon train under the command of Henry's friend, William Shaw. Henry bought a large wagon and some strong oxen to pull it. Naomi loaded the wagon with flour, sugar, coffee, cornmeal, and dried fruit. She packed quilts and clothing, and a few tools and cooking pots. With these meager supplies, they set out on a 2,000-mile (3,219 km) journey to a new home.

3

Life on the trail was difficult. The oxen had to work hard to pull the heavy wagon, so the children mostly had to walk. Cold spring rains soaked their clothing. Meals had to be cooked over open fires. At night, each person rolled up in a blanket and slept inside or under the wagon. But it was a grand adventure, and there were moments of fun. On clear evenings, everyone gathered around campfires to play instruments and sing. And, on May 30, a joyful event came to the Sager family—a new baby girl was born.

4

Unfortunately, Naomi was weak and ill from the baby's birth. Travel was hard for her. Then, to make matters worse, Catherine had a terrible accident. She was riding with Henry on the front seat of the wagon and decided to jump down. As she jumped, her dress caught on an ax handle. She was thrown beneath the wheel of the heavy wagon. The wheel rolled across her leg, breaking it badly. A kind doctor, Dr. Dagon, helped Henry set Catherine's leg.

5

THE STORY OF THE SAGERS

A few weeks later, Henry became dreadfully ill. He had a very high fever. Naomi tried to help Henry, but there was nothing she could do. After a few days of suffering, Henry died. His friends and family buried him beside the trail and moved on. The effort of caring for Henry in his illness and her grief at his death took a toll on Naomi. Already weak, she too became seriously ill. Before she died, she gathered her children together to tell them good-bye. She made John and Francis promise that they would take care of the girls and keep the family together.

6

Now the children were left alone with no parents and no home. But they did have some good friends. William Shaw and his wife, Sally, fed the children and looked after them. Dr. Dagon drove their wagon. Other women from the wagon train took turns caring for the newborn baby. The Shaws decided to take the children to the mission at Waiilatpu. Everyone hoped that Narcissa and Marcus would take them in.

7

After two more months of hard travel, the wagons pulled up to the door of the mission. Narcissa came out of the house to greet the children. The children were glad their difficult journey was over, but frightened and confused. The Whitmans were complete strangers to them. But Marcus and Narcissa welcomed them with warm smiles and took them into the house.

8

As time passed, the Sager children grew comfortable in their new home. The baby and the younger girls adapted quickly. They remembered little about their parents and were happy to have a home. The older children, especially the boys, had a more difficult time. But gradually, they too began to feel at home at Waiilatpu. For the next three years, life was good for the Sager children.

9

EMC 3704 • Moving West • ©2003 by Evan-Moor Corp.

THE STORY OF THE SAGERS

This was a busy time at the mission. The Oregon Trail passed right by the mission door. Many of the emigrants needed help. They needed food, medicine, and a place to rest. This placed a heavy burden on Marcus and Narcissa, who already had enough to do in caring for their children and for the Native Americans near the mission.

10

Some of the Native Americans were very unhappy about the newcomers. Often they were sick with measles and other diseases when they arrived. They spread these diseases to the Native Americans. When white people became ill, Marcus would doctor them, and they usually recovered. Though Marcus tried to help the Native Americans, they almost always died.

11

Many of the Native Americans understood that Marcus was trying to help. But others blamed him. They thought that if they could get rid of Marcus and the mission, the white people would stay away. On November 29, 1847, a small band of Cayuse attacked the mission. They killed Marcus, Narcissa, and all the men they could find, including John and Francis Sager. The Sager girls were taken prisoner. After a month of captivity, they were finally released.

12

Louise Sager died from illness during the captivity. Catherine, Elizabeth, and Matilda survived to tell their amazing story. It is a story of tragedy, heartbreak, and courage. It is a story that has become an enduring piece of the history of the westward movement.

13

Pocket 5

ON THE
OREGON TRAIL

FAST FACTS

Prepare the bookmark about the emigrants on the Oregon Trail, following the directions on page 2. Students read and share the interesting facts about life on the trail. Use the Fast Facts for a quick review during transition times throughout the day.

ABOUT

Reproduce this page for students. Read and discuss the important information to remember. Use this page as a reference guide for the activities in the pocket. Incorporate library and multimedia resources that are available.

ACTIVITIES

Children were often allowed to choose only one small, treasured possession to bring with them on the overland journey. Have students draw and write about what possession they would choose to take and why. Students slip their treasured possession into a "trunk" for safekeeping.

Everything on the frontier had to be used and used again. Scraps of fabric were sewn together to create coverlets that warmed the pioneers' hearts as well as their bodies. Students make their own quilt squares filled with memories.

Read about the games children played on the long journey. Then have students play the popular game of Bingo to test their knowledge of emigrants traveling west.

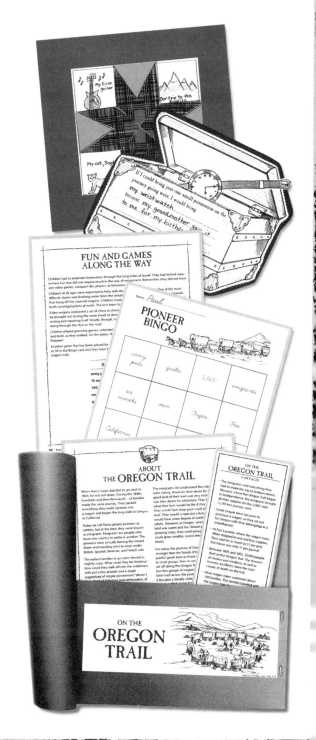

ON THE
OREGON TRAIL

ON THE
OREGON TRAIL

FAST FACTS

- The emigrants sold everything they had to make the trip to Independence, Missouri, where the Oregon Trail began. In Independence, the emigrants bought all their supplies for the 2,000-mile (3,219 km) journey west.

- Some people were too poor to purchase a wagon, so they set out for Oregon with their belongings in a wheelbarrow.

- At Fort Laramie, where the wagon trains often stopped to rest and buy supplies, flour sold for as much as $1 per pint, but bacon was only 1¢ per pound!

- Between 1835 and 1855, 10,000 people died on the Oregon Trail. The diseases of cholera and smallpox, as well as firearms accidents, were the main causes of death on the trail.

- Most wagon trains contained about 100 families. The families traveled with the wagon train for nearly six months, crossing the country.

- A typical wagon could hold about 2,500 pounds (1,134 kg) of supplies.

- Wagon trains covered about 15 miles (24 km) a day. At night, the wagons would form a circle that served as a pen for the livestock.

- Emigrants traveled on many trails west. The Oregon Trail is the most famous. However, there was also the California Trail, the Mormon Trail, and the Santa Fe Trail, all leading emigrants west.

ABOUT
THE OREGON TRAIL

When Henry Sager decided to go west in 1844, he was not alone. During the 1840s, hundreds—and then thousands—of families made the same journey. They packed everything they could squeeze into a wagon and began the long walk to Oregon or California.

Today we call these people pioneers or settlers, but at the time, they were known as emigrants. Emigrants are people who leave one country to settle in another. The pioneers were actually leaving the United States and traveling west to areas under British, Spanish, Mexican, and French rule.

The earliest families to go were viewed as slightly crazy. What could they be thinking? How could they walk off into the wilderness with just a few animals and a single wagonload of simple possessions? Weren't they afraid of lightning and rattlesnakes, of bears and hunger and Indians? Didn't they know they would never see their loved ones again?

The emigrants did understand the risks they were taking. However, their desire for fresh, good land of their own was very strong. So was their desire for adventure. They knew what their lives would be like if they stayed. They would farm their poor small plots of land. They would scrape out a living. They would have some degree of comfort and safety. However, in Oregon, where the land was sweet and the climate perfect for growing crops, they could prosper. They could grow wealthy. Grand dreams filled their heads.

For many, the promise of Oregon was stronger than the bonds of home. They said painful good-byes to those staying behind. In small groups, then in vast numbers, they set off along the Oregon Trail. After the first few groups of wagons, this trail was a faint track across the prairie. Before long, it became a deeply rutted road. So many wagons rolled across it that, even today, the ruts are still visible in many places.

ONE SPECIAL THING

The wagons were full to the brim with necessities for the journey. Every spare inch was filled with things that might help the family survive. Their parents often told children that they could choose only one small possession to bring along on the journey.

Children at that time did not have many toys, but they usually had a few cherished items. A boy might have a pocketknife, some marbles, and a collection of rocks, feathers, and other found items. A girl probably had a rag or cornhusk doll or two, a sampler she had stitched, and perhaps a small box of paints or a diary.

Have students choose one small treasured possession they would take on the journey going west. Students make the treasure to slip into a trunk for safekeeping.

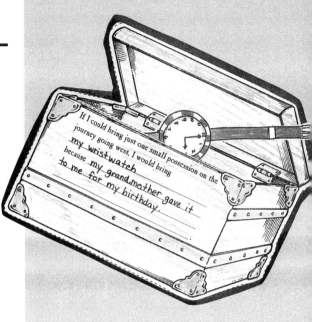

STEPS TO FOLLOW

1. Discuss what special things pioneer children brought along on the trail.

2. Have students choose one special treasure they would bring along on the trail.

3. Direct students to draw, color, and cut out a picture of their treasure using the white construction paper.

4. Instruct students to cut out the trunk pattern. Then they cut the slit in the trunk.

5. Have students glue the trunk to the brown construction paper, making sure the slit is not glued down. Have them cut around the trunk shape.

6. Direct students to write about their possession using the lines provided on the trunk.

7. Have students place their treasure inside the trunk for safekeeping.

MATERIALS

- page 46, reproduced for each student
- 6" x 9" (15 x 23 cm) white construction paper
- 9" x 12" (23 x 30.5 cm) brown construction paper
- pencil
- crayons or marking pens
- scissors
- glue

ONE SPECIAL THING

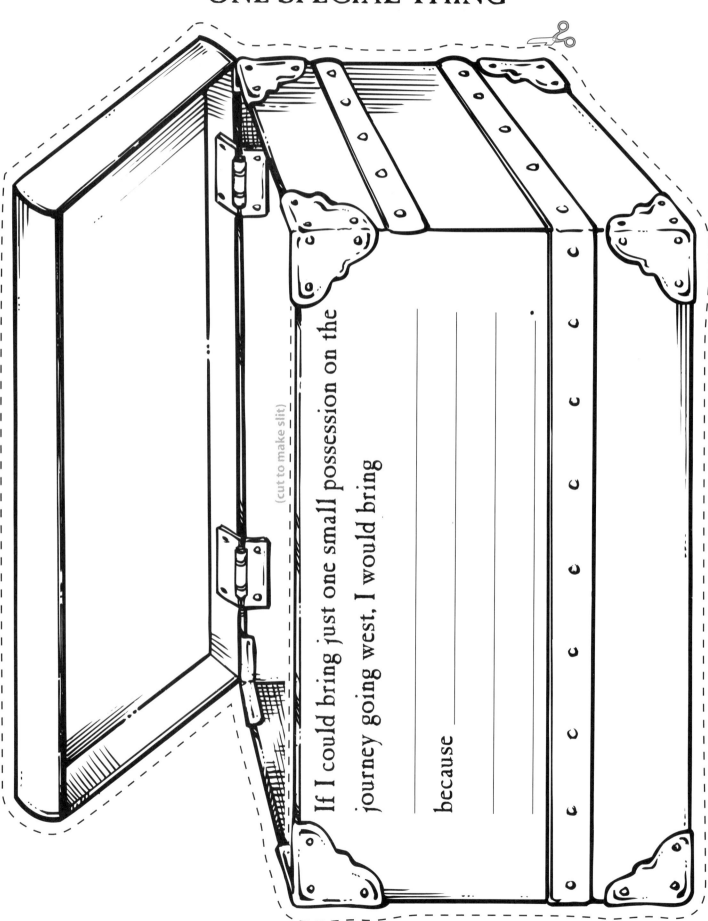

(cut to make slit)

If I could bring just one small possession on the

journey going west, I would bring

because _____

EMC 3704 • Moving West • ©2003 by Evan-Moor Corp.

MEMORY QUILTS

One of the most treasured possessions needed on the trails heading west was the family's patchwork quilt. The quilt was made from scraps of the family's clothing, and each square held a special memory.

Students make their own quilt squares filled with special memories.

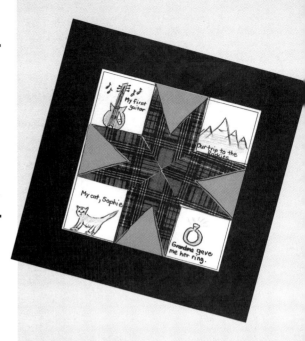

STEPS TO FOLLOW

1. Have students write and draw about four special happy memories in the four corners of the star quilt pattern. Ideas such as a favorite vacation, birth of a sibling, a birthday party, or receiving a new pet could be used.

2. Direct students to cut out the quilt piece templates.

3. Use the two templates on the bottom of page 48 to trace onto scraps of colorful paper. Have students cut out the pieces and glue them onto the star quilt.

4. Have students cut out the completed quilt square and glue it to the construction paper square for added durability.

5. Share the quilt squares in class. You may choose to hang all the quilt squares together to make one giant class quilt.

MATERIALS

- page 48, reproduced for each student
- 9" x 9" (23 x 23 cm) construction paper
- pencil
- crayons or marking pens
- scraps of colored paper, wrapping paper, or wallpaper samples
- scissors
- glue

STAR QUILT PATTERN

Everything on the frontier had to be used and used again. Scraps of fabric were saved from baby clothes, aprons, wedding dresses, and shirts. These were sewn together to create coverlets that warmed the pioneers' hearts as well as their bodies. Each piece of the quilt contained a memory of a special person or event.

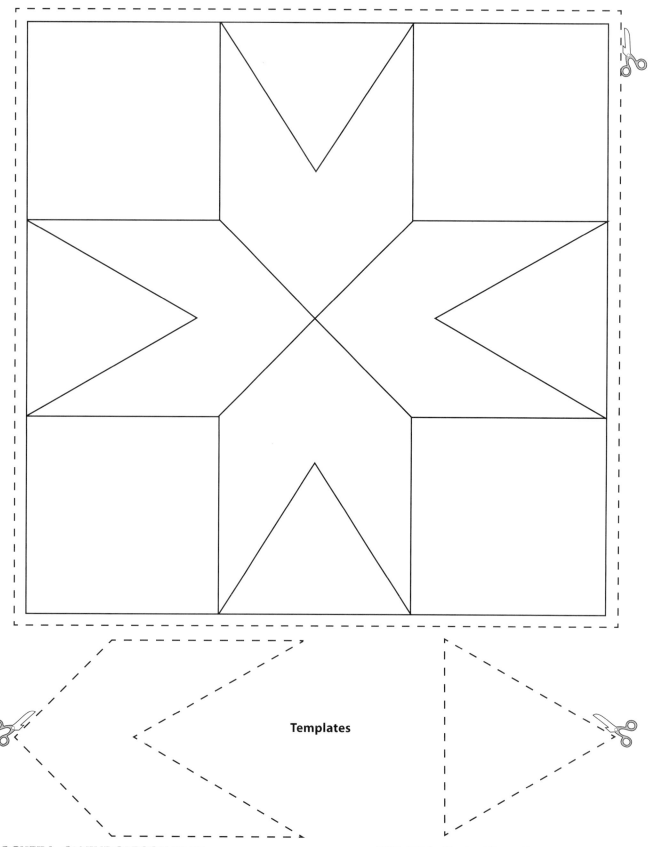

Templates

   EMC 3704 • *Moving West* • ©2003 by Evan-Moor Corp.

FUN AND GAMES ALONG THE WAY

Pioneer children had to make their own kind of fun as they traveled along on the wagon trains. Students read about games pioneer children played. Then they test their pioneer knowledge when they play Bingo.

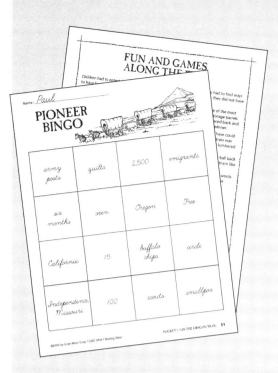

STEPS TO FOLLOW

1. Read and discuss the information about what games children played while traveling on the wagon trains.

2. Then give each student a Bingo card and 16 game markers.

3. Have students randomly write the 15 words listed on page 50 (and the "FREE" square) on their game boards.

4. Play the game with students. Remind them to shout out "Bingo" when they have answered four questions correctly either horizontally, vertically, or diagonally.

MATERIALS

- pages 50 and 51, reproduced for each student
- 16 game markers

Questions and Answers for Bingo

1. The earliest pioneers called themselves ___. *(emigrants)*

2. A lot of emigrants followed a trail heading to the territory of ___. *(Oregon)*

3. How long did it take most emigrants to make the 2,000-mile (3,219 km) journey to Oregon? *(six months)*

4. Where did the Oregon Trail begin? *(Independence, Missouri)*

5. Wagon trains traveled about ___ miles (km) a day. *(15 miles or 24 km)*

6. Ten thousand people died along the Oregon Trail. What was one of the causes of death? *(smallpox)*

7. Women made special ___ from the family's old clothing. *(quilts)*

8. A typical wagon could hold about ___ pounds (kg) of supplies. *(2,500 pounds or 1,134 kg)*

9. At night the wagon train would form a ___ that served as a pen for the livestock. *(circle)*

10. Children flung dry ___ as Frisbees, but the more practical use for them was to build fires. *(buffalo chips)*

11. Wagon trains had about ___ families traveling together. *(100)*

12. Many emigrants left the Oregon Trail and headed southwest to ___. *(California)*

13. Covered wagons sometimes used a team of ___ to pull them. *(oxen)*

14. ___ rode ahead of the wagon train to look for water and places to camp. *(scouts)*

15. Wagon trains stopped at ___ like Fort Laramie to rest and get more supplies. *(army posts)*

FUN AND GAMES ALONG THE WAY

Children had to entertain themselves through the long miles of travel. They had to find ways to have fun that did not require much in the way of equipment. Remember, they did not have any video games, compact disc players, or television sets!

Children of all ages were expected to help with the chores along the trail. One of the most difficult chores was fetching water from the stream or river to refill the large storage barrels that hung off the covered wagons. Children made a game of this. Two teams raced back and forth carrying buckets of water. The first team to fill the storage barrel was the winner.

A few wagons contained a set of chess or checkers, or perhaps a deck of cards. These could be brought out during the noon break or during a "lay by" day when the wagon train was resting and repairing itself. Mostly, though, fun had to be made up as the wagons lumbered along through the dust or the mud.

Children played guessing games, collected flowers and feathers, or tossed a leather ball back and forth as they walked. On the plains, they might find dry buffalo chips and fling them like Frisbees!

Another game that has been played for many generations is Bingo. Use the following words to fill in the Bingo card and then have fun testing your knowledge of pioneer life on the wagon trails.

BINGO WORDS

army posts	Oregon
15 miles (24 km)	buffalo chips
100	emigrants
smallpox	California
quilts	scouts
2,500 pounds (1,134 kg)	six months
oxen	circle
Independence, Missouri	"FREE"

EMC 3704 • *Moving West* • ©2003 by Evan-Moor Corp

Name: _____

PIONEER BINGO

Pocket 6

THE NATIVE AMERICAN STRUGGLE

FAST FACTS

Prepare the bookmark about the Native American struggle, following the directions on page 2. Students read and share the interesting information about how life changed for the Native Americans. Use the Fast Facts for a quick review during transition times throughout the day.

ABOUT

Reproduce this page for students. Read and discuss the important information to remember. Use this page as a reference guide for the activities in the pocket. Incorporate library and multimedia resources that are available.

ACTIVITIES

Read and discuss two tragic events: the Trail of Tears and the Long Walk. Have students compare and contrast the removals of the Cherokee and the Navajo tribes using a Venn diagram.

Learn about the important relationship between the Plains Indians and the buffalo. Students create a portrait of the buffalo using tissue paper collage techniques.

Students create a three-panel picture featuring wise words from three different Native American tribes.

THE NATIVE AMERICAN STRUGGLE

THE NATIVE AMERICAN STRUGGLE

©2003 by Evan-Moor Corp. • EMC 3704

THE NATIVE AMERICAN STRUGGLE

FAST FACTS

- When the Europeans arrived in North America, there were about 300 different Native American nations on the continent. There were about two million Native Americans in the 1800s.

- In the early 1800s, Tecumseh, a Shawnee chief, warned Native American nations that if they did not band together to fight the westward movement, the Native Americans' way of life would be destroyed.

- The American Indians traded horses, metal goods, and eventually guns with the Europeans. But when the pioneers came in numbers, conflicts arose.

- Europeans called the Plains Dakota Nation the Sioux. The Dakota did not like this name because it means "enemy" in the language of a rival tribe (the Ojibwa).

- In the early 1800s, there were about 60 million buffalo in North America. By the end of the 1800s, there were only about 12 million left. And by 1900, there were only a few thousand buffalo left.

- The American painter George Catlin explored the West from 1830 to 1836. His goal was to record the daily life of the 48 Native American tribes in the region. He made over 500 paintings and sketches of Native Americans in the West.

- The Europeans called Native American shamans "medicine men." Shamans used ceremonies to help people reject sickness. They carried bags of natural herbs to help heal people.

ABOUT
THE NATIVE AMERICAN STRUGGLE

When settlers began to spread across the West, they brought their own cultures with them. These cultures were different from the cultures of the Native Americans.

The settlers were mostly farmers. They cleared trees, planted crops, and built fences. Of course, the lands these settlers claimed for their farms were lands that had long been home to a variety of Native American tribes. While some settlers were sympathetic to the Native Americans, most were not. Many settlers thought the Native Americans were simply in the way, and that they should make room for the settlers.

This was accomplished in several different ways. Some lands were bought from the Native Americans, but this process had some problems. Many Native Americans did not have the same understanding of property ownership and were therefore often cheated. Tribal structures varied, and the U.S. government would make deals without the knowledge or consent of a tribe as a whole.

Sometimes the government made treaties with the Native Americans, granting them the rights to certain lands if they would withdraw from a particular area. The treaties were often signed under threat of violence. Many treaties were broken when more land was needed, or when the land "given" to

Native Americans turned out to be more valuable than expected. In the worst cases, Native Americans were rounded up and forced to leave their homes to make room for the settlers.

In spite of all these injustices, the Native Americans survived the struggle. Today there are several hundred tribes living within the borders of the United States. There are 2.5 million Native Americans in the United States and Canada. They live on reservations and in towns and cities throughout the United States. Native American people work to retain their tribal languages and customs.

   EMC 3704 • *Moving West* • ©2003 by Evan-Moor Corp.

CULTURES IN CONFLICT

Many Native Americans were displaced when the pioneers started to settle the western frontier. The Trail of Tears is the tragic journey the proud Cherokee Nation took when they were forced to move from their homeland in Tennessee to Oklahoma. The other sad event is called the Long Walk, which is how the proud Navajo Nation was forced to move from their beloved home in northern Arizona and New Mexico to a desolate reservation in eastern New Mexico.

Students read about the two tragic stories, and then compare and contrast the events using a Venn diagram.

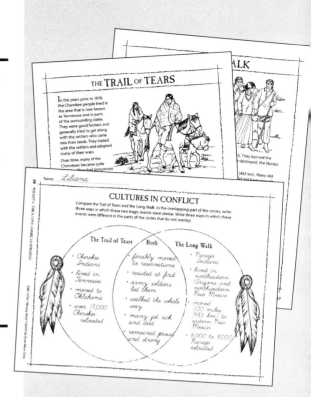

STEPS TO FOLLOW

1. Read and discuss "The Trail of Tears" and "The Long Walk" (on pages 56 and 57) with students.

2. Have students fill out the Venn diagram on page 58, noting the similarities and differences between the two tragic events in American history. You may choose to do this activity as a class, in small groups, or in pairs.

3. A copy of the completed Venn diagram is provided below to use as reference.

MATERIALS

• pages 56–58, reproduced for each student

• pencil

VENN DIAGRAM
Answer Key

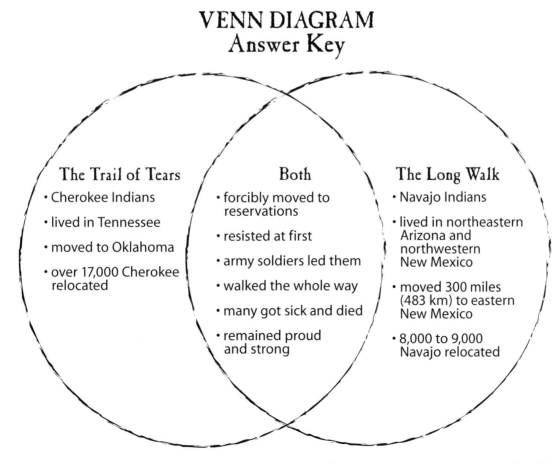

The Trail of Tears
• Cherokee Indians
• lived in Tennessee
• moved to Oklahoma
• over 17,000 Cherokee relocated

Both
• forcibly moved to reservations
• resisted at first
• army soldiers led them
• walked the whole way
• many got sick and died
• remained proud and strong

The Long Walk
• Navajo Indians
• lived in northeastern Arizona and northwestern New Mexico
• moved 300 miles (483 km) to eastern New Mexico
• 8,000 to 9,000 Navajo relocated

THE TRAIL OF TEARS

In the years prior to 1838, the Cherokee people lived in the area that is now known as Tennessee and in parts of the surrounding states. They were good farmers and generally tried to get along with the settlers who came into their lands. They traded with the settlers and adopted many of their ways.

Over time, many of the Cherokees became quite wealthy. They had prosperous farms and large homes. They built schools and businesses. While some of the Cherokee people resisted the white man's ways, many of them wanted to get along. They felt they could live side by side with their new neighbors.

However, no matter how hard they tried, it was never enough. Some greedy white people wanted to take the rich farms of the Cherokees. They did not want to live with Native American people, no matter how peaceful and agreeable they might be. They began to push for the removal of the Cherokees from their homes.

Andrew Jackson was the president of the United States at this time. He wanted to move the Native Americans out of the way. He wanted white settlers and farmers to have all the land. He ordered the Cherokees to leave their homes and prepare to move to reservations in present-day Oklahoma.

About 250 Cherokees did as they were told, but most of them—17,000 strong—refused. The government sent soldiers to their homes and forced them out. The soldiers took the Cherokees to camps. Here they were packed together. They were not fed well. They did not have good shelters. Many got sick and died.

After a few months in the camps, the Cherokee people were forced to march the 1,000 miles (1,609 km) to Oklahoma. They did not have warm clothes or blankets. They were given little food, and it was of poor quality. Many more of the people died.

The route the Cherokee followed to Oklahoma became known as the Trail of Tears. In all, about one-fourth of the Cherokee Nation perished in this shameful and painful chapter of U.S. history.

 EMC 3704 • Moving West • ©2003 by Evan-Moor Corp.

THE LONG WALK

The Cherokee were not the only people to suffer a mass removal. The Navajo met a similar fate. In 1864 the United States Army, under the command of Colonel Kit Carson, was sent to move the Navajo people out of their homes and onto a reservation over 300 miles (483 km) away. The Navajos were to walk from northeastern Arizona and northwestern New Mexico to a barren piece of land in eastern New Mexico.

At first, the Navajo refused to move. They hid in a canyon area called Canyon de Chelly. The army destroyed their crops and livestock. They burned the villages and killed many people. Since their food supplies were destroyed, the Navajo eventually were convinced to go to the reservation.

Some 8,000 to 9,000 Navajos were forced to walk the 300 miles (483 km). Many did not survive the march. The weather was cold, and the Navajos did not have enough clothes, blankets, or food. Those who could not keep up were beaten and sometimes killed. Overall, 200 people died on the march.

The area chosen by the U.S. government for the reservation was barren and drab. This area was out of the way of advancing settlers. The water was very bad and made the people sick. There were few trees, so firewood was scarce. The land was so poor that little would grow. Thousands of Navajo people endured four years of misery and starvation at this reservation, called Bosque Redondo. Many Navajo people consider that Bosque Redondo was more of a prison camp than a reservation.

Navajo leaders talked with men from the United States government. Barboncito was one of these leaders. He explained how terrible the living conditions were for his people. He insisted that the Navajos needed to return to their homelands. They needed to live between the four sacred mountains that marked the boundaries of their spiritual and physical home.

At last, the United States government agreed to let the Navajo people go home. General Tecumseh Sherman came to the reservation. He brought with him a new treaty promising to give the Navajo people corn seed, sheep, and cattle, and to build schools for their children. However, most importantly, the new treaty said that the Navajos could go back to the lands that they loved.

CULTURES IN CONFLICT

Compare the Trail of Tears and the Long Walk. In the overlapping part of the circles, write three ways in which these two tragic events were similar. Write three ways in which these events were different in the parts of the circles that do not overlap.

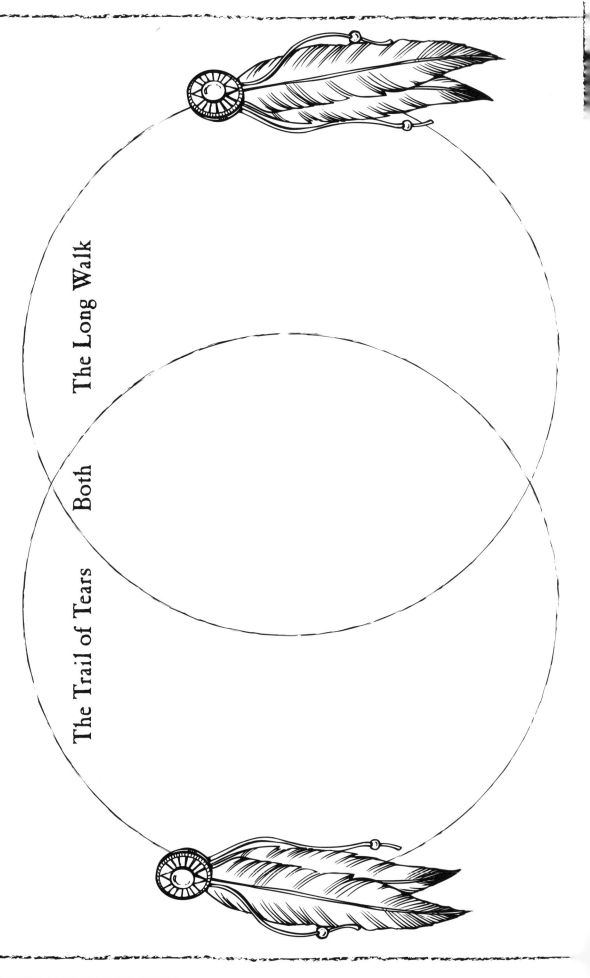

The Long Walk

Both

The Trail of Tears

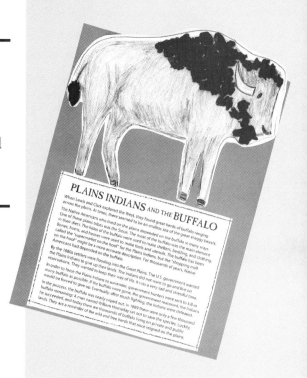

PLAINS INDIANS
AND THE BUFFALO

Students read about the Plains Indians and the buffalo (also called American bison). Then the students make a portrait of this great shaggy beast.

STEPS TO FOLLOW

1. Share the information about the Plains Indians and the buffalo on page 60.

2. Have students study the picture of the buffalo. Point out the large head and high shoulders of this animal.

3. Direct students to glue the information to the bottom half of the green construction paper.

4. Students make an outline of a buffalo on the white construction paper, making the buffalo as large as possible.

5. Have students color the buffalo and then use tissue paper squares to add texture to the furry head and shoulders of the buffalo. Students pour about a teaspoon of glue onto a paper plate. Students squeeze a square of tissue paper into a wad, dip it lightly into the glue (only a little is needed) and press it onto the buffalo.

6. After the glue has dried, instruct students to cut out the buffalo and glue it to the top of the green construction paper. Note: The buffalo will extend slightly above the green construction paper.

MATERIALS

- page 60, reproduced for each student
- 9" x 12" (23 x 30.5 cm) green construction paper
- 9" x 12" (23 x 30.5 cm) white construction paper
- black and different shades of brown tissue paper, cut into 1" (2.5 cm) squares
- scissors
- crayons
- glue
- paper plate
- pictures of buffalo, if available

PLAINS INDIANS AND THE BUFFALO

When Lewis and Clark explored the West, they found great herds of buffalo ranging across the plains. At times, there seemed to be an endless sea of the great shaggy beasts.

The Native Americans who lived on the plains depended on the buffalo in many ways. One of these plains tribes was the Sioux. The meat of the buffalo was the main element in their diet. The hides of the buffalo were used to make shelters, bedding, and clothing. Bones, horns, and hooves were used to make tools and utensils. The buffalo has been called the "supermarket on the hoof" for the Plains Indians, but the "shopping mall on the hoof" might be a more accurate description. For thousands of years, Native Americans had depended on the buffalo.

By the 1880s settlers were flooding into the Great Plains. The U.S. government wanted the Plains Indians to give up their lands. The Indians did not want to go and live on reservations. They wanted to keep their way of life. It was a very sad and stressful time.

In order to force the Plains Indians to surrender, government hunters were sent to kill as many buffalo as possible. If the buffalo were gone, the government reasoned, the Indians would be forced to give up. Eventually, after much fighting, the Indians were defeated.

In the process, the buffalo was nearly wiped out. In 1889 there were only a few thousand buffalo remaining! A man named William Hornaday set out to save the species. Luckily, he succeeded, and today there are thousands of buffalo living on private and public lands. They are a reminder of the wild and free herds that once reigned on the plains.

Buffalo (American bison)

   EMC 3704 • Moving West • ©2003 by Evan-Moor Corp.

WORDS OF WISDOM

Read the quotations from the three Native American tribes to the students. Have students illustrate the quotations.

STEPS TO FOLLOW

1. Give students the three quotations. Discuss the quotations with students, and elicit student thinking about their meanings. Point out the tribes where each quotation originated. Note the discussions of each tribe in this pocket.

2. Tell students to fold the black construction paper into thirds to make three 6″ x 6″ (15 x 15 cm) panels.

3. Have students fold and cut the white paper into fourths. They glue one white panel (lengthwise) to the top of each of the three black construction paper panels. Note: You will have one white panel left over.

4. Instruct students to cut out and glue each quotation beneath one of the white panels.

5. Direct students to draw illustrations on the white panels to symbolize the quotations.

MATERIALS

- page 61 (bottom half), reproduced for each student
- 6″ x 18″ (15 x 45.5 cm) black construction paper
- 8″ x 11″ (21.5 x 28 cm) white copy paper
- pencil
- colored pencils or fine-tip marking pens
- scissors
- glue

Have patience. All things change in due time. Wishing cannot bring autumn glory or cause winter to cease.

— Cherokee

With all things and in all things, we are relatives.

—Sioux

Walk on a rainbow trail; walk on a trail of song, and all about you will be beauty. There is a way out of every dark mist, over a rainbow trail.

—Navajo

Pocket 7

SETTLING THE FAR WEST

FAST FACTS

Prepare the bookmark about settling the Far West, following the directions on page 2. Students read and share the interesting information about the Far West. Use the Fast Facts for a quick review during transition times throughout the day.

ABOUT

Reproduce this page for students. Read and discuss the important information to remember. Use this page as a reference guide for the activities in the pocket. Incorporate library and multimedia resources that are available.

ACTIVITIES

The settlers heading to the West either rode in Conestogas or Prairie Schooners. Students make a flap book of facts about these covered wagons.

Students read about the famous battle between Mexico and the American settlers in Texas. Students create their own drawing of the Alamo, a symbol of Texan history.

Ranchos were common in California. Life on the ranchos centered on the family, food, and hospitality. Students read about this life and then make enough warm flour tortillas for the whole class.

EMC 3704 • Moving West • ©2003 by Evan-Moor Corp.

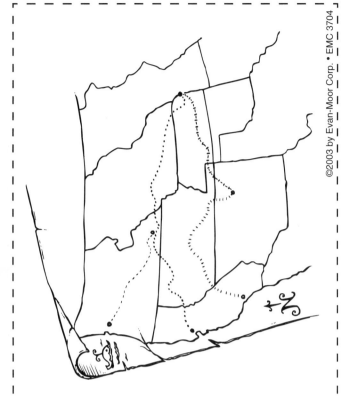

SETTLING THE FAR WEST

SETTLING THE FAR WEST
FAST FACTS

- The settlers going to the Southwest on the Santa Fe Trail used Conestoga wagons. Another nickname for a Conestoga wagon was "stogie." The term *stogie* came from the long, strong cigars smoked by the wagon masters.

- In 1821 William Becknell, a Missouri trader, was the first to take his mule train on the route that later became known as the Santa Fe Trail.

- Those settlers bound for California headed southwest of the Oregon Trail, on the California Trail. They had to go across the Nevada desert. They had a difficult journey crossing the Sierra Nevada Mountains in wagons.

- William Barrett Travis was the commander of the Alamo. He was the first man to fall in the battle. Travis was only 26 years old.

- Davy Crockett was 50 years old when he died at the Alamo.

- In 1848 the signing of the Treaty of Guadalupe Hidalgo ended the Mexican War. The United States gained more than 525,000 square miles (1,360,000 square km) of land. Those lands included California, Nevada, Utah, most of Arizona, and parts of Colorado, New Mexico, and Wyoming.

- In the Southwest, Spanish names are all over the map! Santa Fe, Los Angeles, Amarillo, and San Francisco are just a few of the many American cities with Spanish names.

ABOUT
SETTLING THE FAR WEST

Some of the earliest emigrants to venture across the Mississippi River did not head to Oregon and the lands in the Northwest. They wanted to settle in the Far West, in the present-day states of New Mexico, Texas, and California.

New Mexico

Traders made their way to Santa Fe, New Mexico, as early as 1821. In Santa Fe, goods could be traded for gold and silver from Mexico. They made the 780-mile (1,255 km) trek from Independence, Missouri, to Santa Fe, New Mexico, along a route that was known as the Santa Fe Trail.

The traders returned to the East with their pockets full of precious metals. They advised people to go to Santa Fe because the Mexican government did not have a firm grip on the region and would not stop American settlers. Settlers journeyed over the Santa Fe Trail to find new homes in the Southwest.

Texas

Large numbers of American settlers moved into Texas during the 1820s. Texas was also owned by Mexico, but Americans asked for permission to establish colonies there. Mexico agreed and gave the Americans some land for their colonies. The settlers poured into Texas in numbers that alarmed the Mexican government. Conflicts began to arise between the Americans and the Mexicans. Eventually, this conflict erupted into warfare. After several terrible battles, the Americans won the war. They established a new country, the Republic of Texas.

California

In 1826 an explorer and mountain man named Jedidiah Smith became the first trailblazer to arrive in California on foot. Over the next several years, adventurers made the difficult journey across the plains and mountains to California.

By the 1840s, wagon trains broke off from the Oregon Trail and headed southwest on the California Trail. Emigrants began to settle in California's inviting valleys. They wanted California to be part of the United States and offered to buy the land from Mexico, but Mexico refused. War broke out in 1846. After the Americans took over Mexico City, Mexico agreed to hand over a large portion of land that now makes up the states of California, Nevada, and Utah. It also includes parts of Wyoming, Colorado, New Mexico, and Arizona.

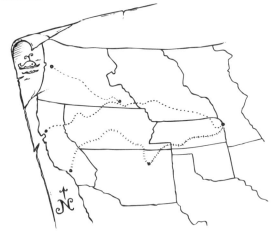

   EMC 3704 • Moving West • ©2003 by Evan-Moor Corp

COVERED WAGON FLAP BOOK

The covered wagon was the best form of transportation for the pioneers heading west. The largest wagon was called the Conestoga. This wagon was used on the Santa Fe Trail. The smaller, lighter Prairie Schooner wagon was used on the Oregon Trail.

Students make a book of facts about these covered wagons.

STEPS TO FOLLOW

1. Discuss that pioneers painted their wagons blue and the wheels red. With their white covers, the wagons looked very patriotic.

2. Have students read about the Conestogas and the Prairie Schooners on page 67.

3. Direct students to choose which wagon they think would have been better as a mode of transportation. Have them write why they chose that style of wagon on the covered wagon form on page 66.

4. Have students color and cut out the covered wagon on page 66 and the two wagon flaps of information on page 67.

5. Direct students to use one of the flaps as a template to cut out another plain white cover. Remind students that pioneers often painted pictures and slogans on the wagon's canvas covering for decoration. Have students do the same on their white covering.

6. Instruct students to staple the three flaps to the top of the covered wagon, making sure their decorated cover is on top.

MATERIALS

- pages 66 and 67, reproduced for each student
- 5½" x 8½" (14 x 21.5 cm) white drawing paper
- red and blue crayons or marking pens
- black marking pen
- scissors
- stapler

COVERED WAGON

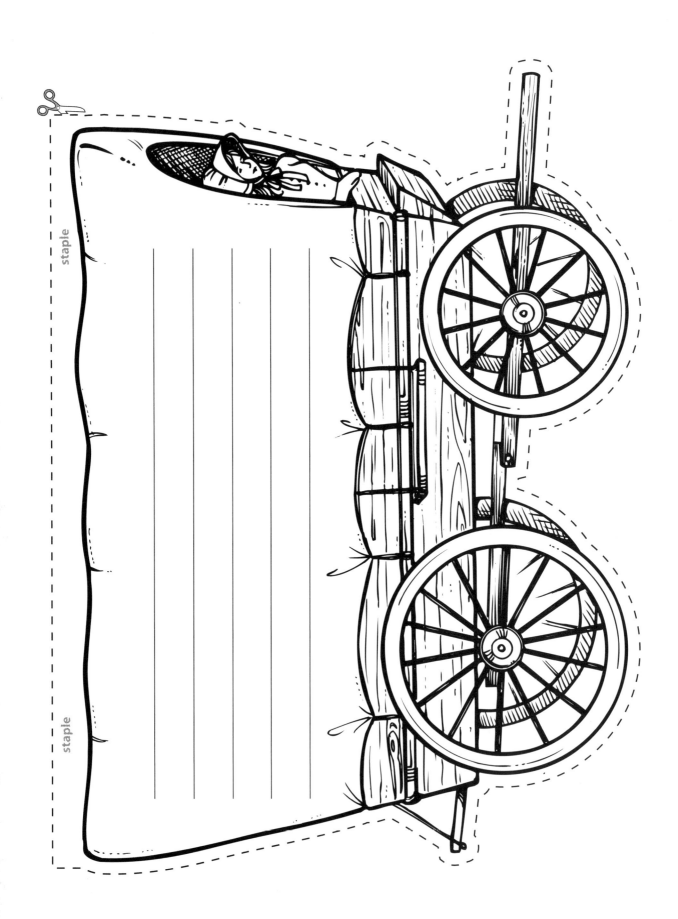

EMC 3704 • Moving West • ©2003 by Evan-Moor Corp.

COVERED WAGON

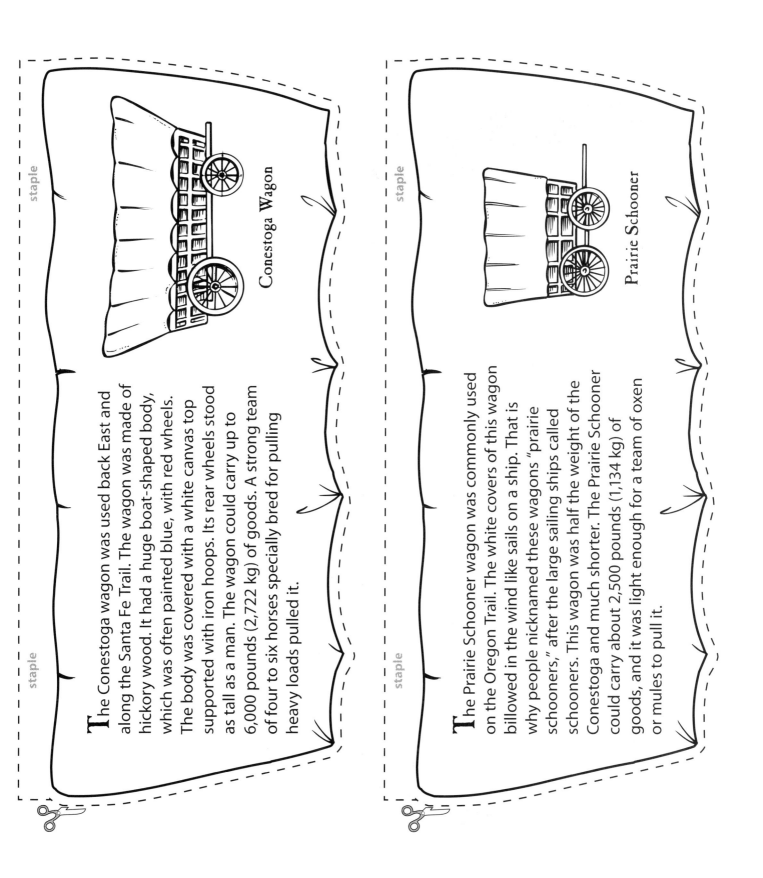

Conestoga Wagon

The Conestoga wagon was used back East and along the Santa Fe Trail. The wagon was made of hickory wood. It had a huge boat-shaped body, which was often painted blue, with red wheels. The body was covered with a white canvas top supported with iron hoops. Its rear wheels stood as tall as a man. The wagon could carry up to 6,000 pounds (2,722 kg) of goods. A strong team of four to six horses specially bred for pulling heavy loads pulled it.

Prairie Schooner

The Prairie Schooner wagon was commonly used on the Oregon Trail. The white covers of this wagon billowed in the wind like sails on a ship. That is why people nicknamed these wagons "prairie schooners," after the large sailing ships called schooners. This wagon was half the weight of the Conestoga and much shorter. The Prairie Schooner could carry about 2,500 pounds (1,134 kg) of goods, and it was light enough for a team of oxen or mules to pull it.

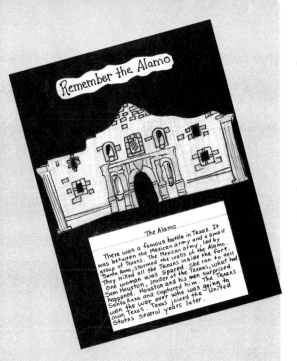

MATERIALS

- page 69, reproduced for each student
- 6" x 9" (15 x 23 cm) white construction paper
- 9" x 12" (23 x 30.5 cm) black construction paper
- 4" x 6" (10 x 15 cm) index card
- pencil
- crayons or colored pencils
- scissors
- glue
- pictures of the Alamo

REMEMBER THE ALAMO

Students read about a famous battle between Mexico and the American settlers in Texas, known as the Alamo. Then students create their own drawings of this symbol of Texan history.

STEPS TO FOLLOW

1. Read about and discuss the famous battle on page 69. Ask students to think about why the Alamo is so important in the history of Texas.

2. Direct students to draw an outline of the Alamo on white construction paper. Have students color the Alamo. Encourage them to add details using the picture of the Alamo on page 69 as a guide.

3. Instruct students to cut out the drawing and mount it on black construction paper.

4. Then have students write a paragraph on the index card, describing the battle at the Alamo. Students glue the index card to their picture of the Alamo. Then they add the title "Remember the Alamo."

REMEMBER THE ALAMO

The Alamo

One famous battle between Mexico and the American settlers in Texas is known as the Alamo. Texan troops attacked the town of San Antonio, and the Mexicans surrendered. This made the president of Mexico, Santa Anna, very angry. He sent a large army to crush the Texan troops. The Texan troops were a small group of less than 200. They hid inside an old, crumbling mission building known as the Alamo. Young William Travis—only 26 years old—was in command.

He sent out a plea for help, but it was too late. Early on the morning of March 6, 1836, Santa Anna's troops stormed the walls of the Alamo. All of the men inside were killed. Santa Anna spared a few women and children. One of these women was Susanna Dickenson. Santa Anna sent Susanna to the leader of the Texans, Sam Houston, to tell him what had happened at the Alamo. He told her to warn all the Texans that they should give up.

The Texans were grief-stricken and angry when they learned that all the men at the Alamo had been killed. They became more determined than ever to win the war. "Remember the Alamo" became the rallying cry for the Texan troops. A few weeks later, Sam Houston and his men were able to surprise Santa Anna and capture him. The war was over, and the Republic of Texas was born. In 1845, Texas joined the United States, becoming the 28th state in the Union.

Today the Alamo is an important historic landmark in the city of San Antonio. Many tourists visit this site every year. The Alamo has been restored to the way it probably looked in its days as a mission.

MATERIALS

- page 71, reproduced for each student
- two 6" (15 cm) construction paper circles
- scissors
- hole punch
- 12" (30.5 cm) yarn, raffia, or string
- ingredients and equipment needed to make tortillas, as listed on page 71

RANCHO LIFE

For a long time, Mexico and all its lands, including California, were ruled by Spain. The king of Spain gave large tracts of land to Spanish soldiers as rewards for their loyalty. These holdings were called "ranchos." The people who lived on them were called "rancheros." For a time, the rancheros lived very comfortably in California. Life on the ranchos was centered around family, food, and hospitality.

Have students pretend they live on a rancho. They are to rewrite the basic recipe for flour tortillas to make enough for the whole class. Make warm tortillas for the class to enjoy.

STEPS TO FOLLOW

1. Read and discuss the information about rancho life with the students.

2. Tell them they are going to make homemade tortillas.

3. Read the recipe for tortillas. Remind the students that this recipe makes six tortillas. Have them adjust the recipe to make enough for the whole class.

4. In groups of four to six, have students make the tortillas following the recipe.

5. While one group is making their tortillas, have the other students cut out the recipe and information circles. Students glue each of them to the construction paper circles.

6. Direct students to punch holes at the top of each paper circle and tie the two together with yarn, raffia, or string.

RANCHO LIFE

Homes on the ranchos were made of adobe bricks. Sometimes the rancheros were able to use the labor of Native Americans from the nearby missions to help with the construction. The rancho home was usually built around a courtyard, or patio.

To make money, rancheros raised cattle for their hides and tallow. Tallow is the fat from cattle. This fat was used to make candles and soap. The hides were used to make leather products. Piles of hides and large blocks of tallow were carried to the coast and sold to the captains of trading ships.

Life on the ranchos centered on family, food, and hospitality. Friends and strangers could always find a welcome at any rancho. Food, music, and conversation were plentiful.

The rancho days are only a memory now, but celebrations in many California towns keep alive some of the old Spanish traditions. Visitors to a rancho could expect to have warm, delicious tortillas at every meal.

FLOUR TORTILLAS

Ingredients for flour tortillas:
2 cups (250 g) all-purpose flour
¼ cup (57 g) vegetable shortening
1 tsp. (6 g) salt
½ cup (120 ml) warm water

Other items needed:
electric skillet or griddle, rolling pin, spatula, fork, butter

Blend the flour, shortening, and salt with a fork until fine crumbs form. Slowly stir in water, adding a little more flour if dough is sticky. Turn dough out onto a floured surface and knead until smooth, about 1 minute. Divide dough into 6 pieces and cover with plastic wrap. Roll each piece of dough into an 8- or 9-inch circle.

Cook tortillas one at a time over medium-high heat on an ungreased skillet or griddle, until brown specks appear. Repeat on other side. Serve with butter.

Makes 6 tortillas.

Pocket 8

THE GOLD RUSH

FAST FACTS

The Gold Rush..............................**page 73**
Prepare the bookmark about the Gold Rush, following the directions on page 2. Students read and share the interesting information about the Gold Rush. Use the Fast Facts for a quick review during transition times throughout the day.

ABOUT

The Gold Rush..............................**page 74**
Reproduce this page for students. Read and discuss the important information to remember. Use this page as a reference guide for the activities in the pocket. Incorporate library and multimedia resources that are available.

ACTIVITIES

An Exciting Discovery...............**pages 75–77**
The discovery of gold at Sutter's Mill was exciting. Students relive that excitement when they "pan" for gold. They fill out an experiment sheet following the scientific process.

Gold Fever..........................**pages 78 & 79**
Have the students write an acrostic poem from the point of view of a "forty-niner" struck with gold fever, using the poetry form on page 79.

   EMC 3704 • Moving West • ©2003 by Evan-Moor Corp

THE GOLD RUSH

THE GOLD RUSH

FAST FACTS

- In 1848 there were about 20,000 people living in California. Just four years later, there were over 200,000 people living and working in California.

- The number of people who came to the gold fields was estimated at 80,000.

- Prospectors were called "forty-niners" because the Gold Rush began in 1849.

- The miners gave their camps colorful names such as Angels Camp, Poverty Hill, Fiddletown, Last Chance, and Whiskey Flat.

- Prices in gold camps were often sky-high. For example, a single egg might cost $1, while a pound of butter or a loaf of bread could cost as much as $5 or $10!

- Gold rush towns attracted criminals, gamblers, and saloon owners. They were ready to take money from the rich prospectors.

- One of the simplest methods of extracting gold was called panning. The prospector scooped up soil into a metal pan. He swirled water around in the pan. The dirt was washed away, leaving the nuggets of gold at the bottom of the pan.

- By the late 1850s, prospectors had found most of the surface gold. Large mining companies moved in with expensive equipment to extract the deep deposits of gold.

ABOUT
THE GOLD RUSH

Life in early America was not easy for most people. When rumors of gold strikes in California began circulating in 1848, there were many who were willing to listen. This is what they heard:

> "In California, gold nuggets are lying around on the ground, free for the taking!"

> "You can dig gold out of the ground with a teaspoon!"

> "The hills of California are made of gold. There's plenty for everyone!"

Many people wanted to believe that, with just a little luck and effort, they could find enough gold to be rich forever. They set off from farms and towns to head to California. African Americans, both slaves and free, joined the journey west to become miners. The escaped slaves hoped to find enough gold to buy freedom. The miners traveled by ship and by wagon, on horseback or on foot.

Besides the Americans, gold seekers came from other countries. They set off on ships to land in New York. There they joined wagon trains heading west, or they traveled by boat to reach California. One popular route took travelers by boat from the East Coast to Panama. There they would cross the isthmus on mules or in canoes. Once on the other side, they would board a ship that would take them to San Francisco.

Chinese immigrants poured into California, hoping to find wealth and a better life. The other miners often mistreated them. The Chinese set up mining camps. They worked together and were often successful.

Some of these miners found gold, but most were disappointed. Instead of gold, they found rough mining camps, full of crime and wild behavior. The "shanty towns" attracted people ready to take the miners' money. Drinking and gambling were forms of entertainment. Gunfights started over gold claims. There were few laws, and the people in the camps carried out their own kind of justice.

The people found that panning for gold was hard, backbreaking work. Many of these people turned back toward home. Some moved on to new gold and silver strikes. Others stayed to make California their home. They worked for the large mining companies or became farmers and shopkeepers.

The Gold Rush changed California and the West. California filled with settlers and soon grew into the most populous state in the Union.

                                     EMC 3704 • Moving West • ©2003 by Evan-Moor Corp.

AN EXCITING DISCOVERY

In 1848, James Marshall, a carpenter, was building a sawmill for John Sutter when he found a gold nugget. He showed it to John Sutter, who wanted to keep it a secret. Of course, the secret got out and the Gold Rush was on.

Students read about this discovery, and they learn how to pan for gold when they try out a science experiment using everyday objects.

STEPS TO FOLLOW

1. Read the story of how gold was found at Sutter's Mill with students.

2. Have students work in small groups to "pan for gold" following the directions on page 77. You may want to do this experiment outside since it is messy. You may choose to do this as a whole class demonstration, if desired.

3. Instruct each student to fill out the science experiment form on the same page. They are to write the hypothesis, which is their guess or answer to the problem statement. They should also write observations and a conclusion.

4. You may want to reward your students with some extra "gold candy" you have on hand.

MATERIALS

- pages 76 and 77, reproduced for each student
- round pie pan (metal or disposable foil)
- dishpan
- dirt, sand, and small pebbles (gravel)
- bucket of water
- paper towels
- newspapers
- pencil
- Optional: simulated gold (butterscotch candies)

AN EXCITING DISCOVERY

John Sutter was an early resident of California. In 1839 he obtained a large tract of land from the Mexican government. This land was in the Sacramento Valley.

Sutter made the local Native Americans work for him. He built a home and a fort, and bought herds of sheep and cattle. He had vineyards, orchards, and farm fields.

Sutter decided to build a sawmill so that he could cut lumber for his building projects. He hired a man named James Marshall to build this new sawmill. Marshall found a good place to build the mill. It was beside the American River, which would provide power for the mill. Marshall took a crew of men and began to work.

One day, while working on the mill, Marshall saw a small yellow pebble in the river. He picked it up. He noticed that it was very heavy. He tried to break the pebble between two stones, but it would not break. Marshall realized that he had found something very exciting: gold!

Marshall took the nugget to John Sutter. Sutter agreed that the nugget was gold. Surprisingly, he was not very pleased about the discovery. He told Marshall not to tell anyone. He knew if word got out fortune-seekers would swarm over his property, digging for the precious metal.

The secret was impossible to keep. A few people heard the story and came to "Sutter's Mill" and the American River. When they returned to San Francisco with gold dust and nuggets, the Gold Rush was on.

EMC 3704 • Moving West • ©2003 by Evan-Moor Co.

Name: _____

"PANNING FOR GOLD"
Science Experiment

PROBLEM: Does the panning method work to find gold?

HYPOTHESIS: I think _____

_____

MATERIALS

- 1 round pie pan
- 1 cup of gravel
- 1 cup of water
- small measuring cup
- 1 dishpan
- water for cleanup
- paper towels

PROCEDURE

1. Fill the pie pan with the gravel mixture.

2. Add a small amount of water to the pie pan.

3. Gently shake the pie pan back and forth over the dishpan so some of the water flows over the sides, carrying away most of the sand and dirt.

4. Pick up any larger rocks that are left. Set them on a paper towel.

5. Add more water to the pie pan and repeat Steps 3 and 4.

6. Observe the larger rocks you have found.

7. Clean up the pie pan and dirty water for the next group.

OBSERVATIONS

_____

_____

_____

_____

CONCLUSION

_____

_____

_____

GOLD FEVER

When a person was struck by a powerful urge to go to the gold diggings, he was said to have gold fever. Gold fever made sensible people do silly things. Many who caught the fever abandoned their families, their homes, and their reputations in their desperate rush to find gold. They simply couldn't stop themselves. They said the sight of gold made their fingers itch and their feet dance. Some people wasted all their money—and even their health—trying to strike it rich.

Have students write an acrostic poem about gold fever from the point of view of someone who is feeling the frantic urge to join the hunt for gold.

MATERIALS

- page 79, reproduced for each student
- 9" x 12" (23 x 30.5 cm) yellow construction paper
- scratch paper
- pencil
- gold glitter or gold glitter pen
- marking pens
- glue

STEPS TO FOLLOW

1. Brainstorm with students to find words that are associated with the Gold Rush.

2. Have students write an acrostic poem called "Gold Fever" on scratch paper.

3. Direct students to write their final copies on the poem form.

4. Allow students to use gold glitter to outline the letters. Allow to dry.

5. Encourage students to add small pictures to their poem.

6. Have students mount the poem onto the yellow construction paper.

7. Share the acrostic poems in class.

EMC 3704 • Moving West • ©2003 by Evan-Moor Corp.

Name: _____

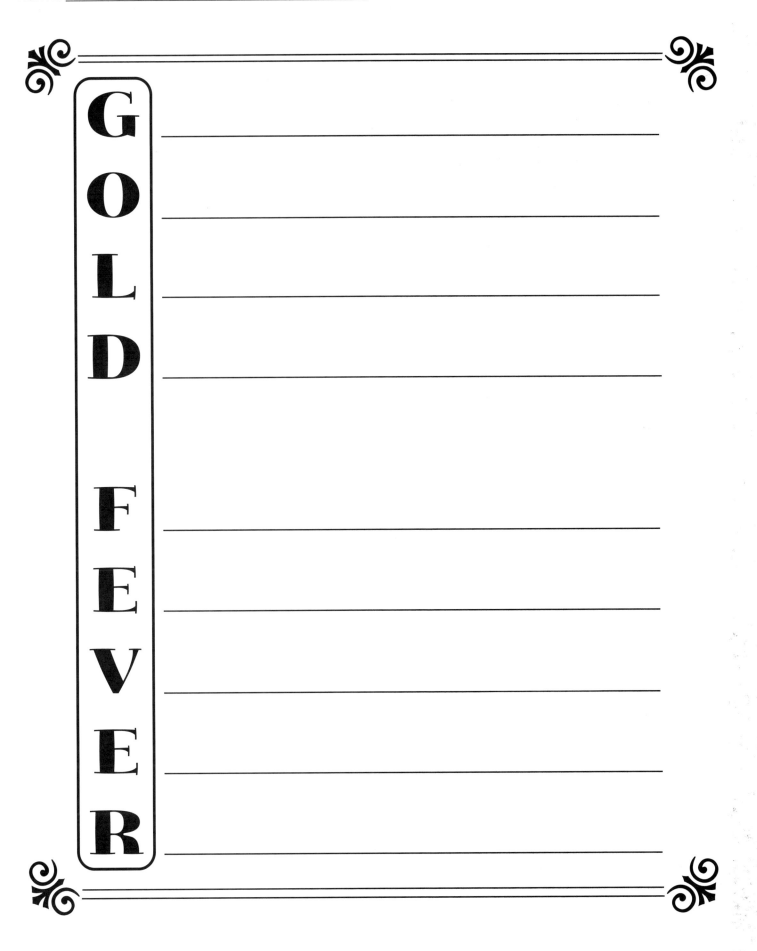

G

O

L

D

F

E

V

E

R

Pocket 9

HOMESTEADING THE GREAT PLAINS

FAST FACTS

Homesteading the Great Plains . . . . **page 81**
Prepare the bookmark about the homesteaders, following the directions on page 2. Students read and share the interesting information about the homesteaders. Use the Fast Facts for a quick review during transition times throughout the day.

ABOUT

Homesteading the Great Plains . . . . **page 82**
Reproduce this page for students. Read and discuss the important information to remember. Use this page as a reference guide for the activities in the pocket. Incorporate library and multimedia resources that are available.

ACTIVITIES

**A Sea of Grass and
an Endless Sky** . . . . **pages 83 & 84**
Students read a poem about the prairie and then they illustrate that poem by painting a lovely picture of the endless prairie.

Benjamin "Pap" Singleton . . . . **pages 85 & 86**
Reproduce these pages for students. Have them read the article on Benjamin "Pap" Singleton on page 85, so students will learn why African Americans chose to leave their homes in the South for a new life in Kansas. After students read the article, they design their own poster encouraging former slaves to leave the South and settle in Kansas. Students may want to glue their posters on a construction paper tree or fence.

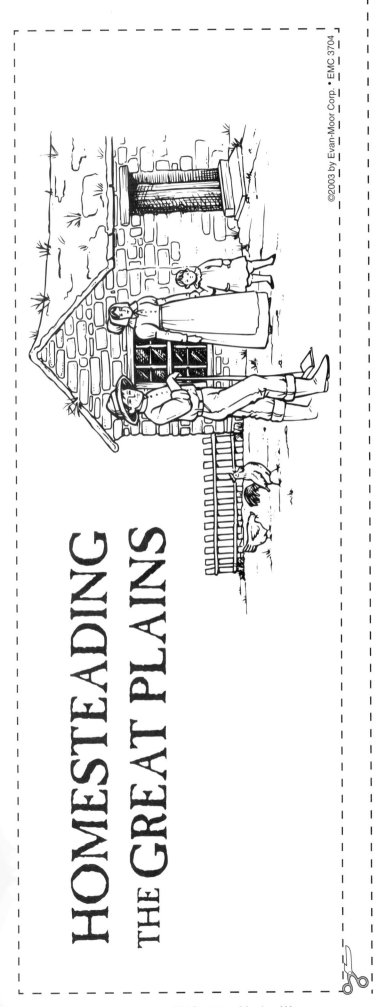

HOMESTEADING
THE GREAT PLAINS

HOMESTEADING THE GREAT PLAINS

FAST FACTS

- Many settlers came to the Great Plains from countries such as Denmark, Norway, Sweden, and Russia. They were called "sodbusters" because they built their homes out of sod. Sod is a top layer of soil containing grass and its roots.

- In the late 1870s, more than 50,000 African Americans left the South to homestead in places like Kansas and Missouri.

- In the springtime, flowers sometimes bloomed on the roofs and walls of the sod houses that were built by settlers on the plains.

- Homesteaders made fires using buffalo or cow chips. Chips were the dried droppings of buffaloes and cows. Children liked to use them as Frisbees.

- Homesteaders had to endure Mother Nature in the form of blizzards, prairie fires, dust storms, thunderstorms, and tornadoes.

- During blizzards, homesteaders had to tie a rope around their waists to go from the house to the barn so they would not get lost in all the freezing snow.

- Swarms of short-horned grasshoppers called locusts sometimes ate a farmer's entire crop! The locusts could be 6 inches (15 cm) deep on the ground!

- The author Laura Ingalls Wilder wrote nine *Little House* books about the prairie life of the homesteaders.

ABOUT
HOMESTEADING THE
GREAT PLAINS

As people traveled overland to California, they had to cross the Great Plains. Most of those early settlers viewed the plains as something of a desert. They had come from the East where there were many trees and rivers. The vast, endless ocean of grass did not seem like a place where people might actually live. To these settlers, the plains were simply part of the route to Oregon or California.

However, in time, Oregon and California began to fill up. People then looked to the Great Plains for settlement. In 1862 the United States government passed the Homestead Act. This act granted 160 acres (65 ha) of land in the Great Plains to any citizen who built a house there and lived in it for at least five years.

Settlers, or homesteaders, began to fan out over these plains. Besides the European immigrants, African Americans from the South made their way to the Great Plains to start new lives as farmers.

The settlers traveled to Kansas, Nebraska, and the Dakotas. They cut chunks of sod out of the earth and used them to build small houses. Sod is the layer of soil that contains the roots of plants. The settlers used plows, knives, and axes to cut strips of sod from the ground. Then they cut these strips into blocks. These chunks of sod were used as bricks. They were stacked, one on top of the other, to create walls. The little bit of precious wood that could be found was used to make a frame for the roof. Sod houses were not ideal, but they provided basic shelters for the settlers.

These homesteaders had to be very tough. They struggled to cut through the tough prairie grasses in order to plant their seeds. They endured dry, dusty summers and long, frigid winters. Wind, hail, and grasshoppers destroyed their crops. Many of them died from the hardships. Many survived and prospered. Today, the prairie states are leading producers of wheat and corn. This region is now called "the nation's breadbasket."

   EMC 3704 • Moving West • ©2003 by Evan-Moor Corp.

A SEA OF GRASS AND AN ENDLESS SKY

Students create an illustration to go with the poem "A Sea of Grass and an Endless Sky."

STEPS TO FOLLOW

1. Have students tape the two pieces of construction paper together lengthwise.

2. Have students dip a sponge into the watercolor paints and press onto the paper to create a lacy effect for the sky.

3. Students paint long grasses across the bottom of the paper. Allow to dry thoroughly.

4. Direct students to fold the paper into six parts as shown.

├── 6" ──┤

5. Instruct students to unfold the paper. They cut out and glue the title and the five stanzas of the poem, one on each section of the paper.

title	first stanza	second stanza	third stanza	fourth stanza	fifth stanza

6. Have students refold the paper so just the title is showing.

7. Students then unfold each section as they read and enjoy the poem.

MATERIALS

- page 84, reproduced for each student
- two 6" x 18" (15 x 45.5 cm) sheets of white construction paper
- scissors
- glue
- transparent tape
- watercolors
- paintbrush
- cup of water
- sponge
- paint cloth or newspapers
- pictures of the prairie

A Sea of Grass and an Endless Sky

Our little house floats on a sea of grass
That bends when the winds pass by.
In rippling shimmers of gold and green
It waves to the endless sky.

Oh, a sea of grass and an endless sky
Are the gifts of a prairie home.
And though they are humble and lowly gifts,
They're the gifts that I call my own.

The meadowlark whistles a happy tune
As he glides through the bright blue air,
And the flowers strewn through the prairie grass
Are like jewels for us to wear.

Oh a meadowlark and a bramble rose
Are the gifts of a prairie home.
And though they are humble and lowly gifts,
They're the gifts that I call my own.

Oh a sea of grass and an endless sky
Are the gifts of a prairie home.
And though you may offer me silver and gold,
You never will tempt me to roam
For I love my prairie home.

—Martha Cheney

   EMC 3704 • Moving West • ©2003 by Evan-Moor Corp.

Note: Reproduce pages 85 and 86 for students to use with the "Benjamin 'Pap' Singleton" activity, as described on page 80.

BENJAMIN "PAP" SINGLETON

After the Civil War, African Americans in the South were freed from slavery, but they were still terribly poor. Benjamin Singleton was one of these former slaves. He wanted to help himself and to help others at the same time. He tried to get a group of black farmers together to buy land in Tennessee, but many white landowners did not want to sell to them.

So "Pap" Singleton decided to lead a group of former slaves to Kansas. This group became known as the Exodusters. (The word *exodus* means "a mass departure from one place to another.") Pap Singleton was sometimes called the "Father of the Exodus."

It was not difficult for Singleton to persuade people to follow him. Though black people in the South were free, they still were not treated well. They were forced to live as second-class citizens. Groups like the Ku Klux Klan rose up during this period. These groups used violence and fear to control and oppress black people. In the late 1870s, more than 50,000 African Americans left the South to settle in places like Kansas and Missouri. Many went on their own. Others followed leaders like Singleton.

Why did Singleton choose Kansas as the best place to go? Kansas had few people and lots of land. Kansas wanted settlers to come and promised good land with rich soil. There were also rumors that former slaves would be given free transportation to Kansas and 40 acres (16 ha) of land, along with plows, seeds, and tools to help them start their farms. Though these rumors were not true, Kansas did offer opportunities for the newcomers.

Singleton tried many things to help his followers. He wanted to help them start their own factories and businesses, but they did not have enough money. When this plan failed, he formed a group to try to help former slaves return to Africa to establish a new homeland. But by this time, Singleton was too old and ill to carry out his plan.

Even though he could not fulfill his dream, Singleton did help many people find better lives. He helped people have confidence in themselves and their own abilities. Many of the families who followed him to Kansas established successful farms. They felt the pride and pleasure of being free to work for themselves for the first time in their lives. Benjamin "Pap" Singleton helped make dreams come true for many people.

BENJAMIN "PAP" SINGLETON

Pap Singleton put up posters in Nashville, Tennessee, urging African Americans to join his exodus to Kansas. Pretend that you are Singleton and use this page to make a poster encouraging others to join you on your journey to Kansas.

Include at least two reasons why people should leave Tennessee and two reasons why they should go to Kansas.

15th of April 1878
Benjamin Singleton, better known as "Pap"
No. 5 North Front Street

EMC 3704 • Moving West • ©2003 by Evan-Moor Corp.

BUILDING THE RAILROADS

FAST FACTS

Prepare the bookmark about the railroads, following the directions on page 2. Students read and share the interesting information about the building of the railroads. Use the Fast Facts for a quick review during transition times throughout the day.

ABOUT

Reproduce this page for students. Read and discuss the important information to remember. Use this page as a reference guide for the activities in the pocket. Incorporate library and multimedia resources that are available.

ACTIVITIES

The race to build the transcontinental railroad was exciting, but dangerous. Students read about this important event in American history. Students create a railroad pop-up, crossing through the American scenery.

Reproduce these two pages for students. They read about the contribution of the Chinese laborers to the building of the railroad. Then they write from different points of view about how the transcontinental railroad affected peoples' lives.

BUILDING THE
RAILROADS

BUILDING THE RAILROADS

FAST FACTS

- Building railroads cost millions of dollars. Railroads were the first big business in America.

- From 1855 to 1905 workers laid 260,000 miles (418,340 km) of track.

- The giant locomotive was nicknamed the "Iron Horse." The first locomotives burned wood, but these were quickly converted to coal. The first locomotives cost from $8,000 to $10,000 to build.

- The first trains to cross the plains were often held up by huge herds of buffalo.

- George Pullman and Ben Field invented the Pullman Palace Car. Palace Cars were sleeper cars that were comfortable and luxurious. They were used by wealthier passengers who could afford them. Ordinary people had to sit on hard wooden benches in day cars on the train.

- When the Central Pacific and the Union Pacific Railroads finally met at Promontory Summit in Utah, ceremonial gold spikes were used to join the two sets of tracks. The spikes were engraved with this prayer: "May God continue the unity of our Country as this Railroad unites the two great Oceans of the world."

- Irish, German, and Chinese immigrants joined freed slaves, Native Americans, and Civil War veterans to build the transcontinental railroad.

ABOUT
BUILDING THE RAILROADS

Theodore Judah had a dream. This brilliant young man was one of the foremost railroad engineers in the land. He had gone to college at the age of 11, and by the time he was 13 years old, he was working as a surveyor for a railroad company. At the age of 25, Judah was sure that a railroad could be built across the formidable Sierra Nevada Mountains.

People thought that Judah was crazy. No one would listen to him. But he refused to give up. He traveled into the Sierras again and again, surveying and planning. He sent his plans to the president of the United States and to Congress. They all laughed at him.

Finding no help from the government, Judah turned to the business community. In 1860 he held a meeting in Sacramento, California, inviting all the wealthy men of the area to listen to him speak. He explained that he could indeed build a railroad through the mountains.

Four of the men who came to that meeting were very interested. Their names were Collis Huntington, Leland Stanford, Charles Crocker, and Mark Hopkins. These men were prosperous storekeepers. They had made their fortunes by selling goods to the miners that had flooded into California during the past decade. They had to use wagons to deliver these goods to the miners. Wagons were slow and expensive. If they could

transport goods by rail, they would save time and money. These men, sometimes called "the Big Four," agreed to finance the railroad.

Judah was excited. At last, he could begin to build his dream. He worked with the Big Four to develop the Central Pacific Railroad Company. Together, they persuaded the government to help pay for the railroad. However, Judah soon learned that his partners were dishonest and were trying to cheat the government. He rushed off to New York to try to find new investors. Unfortunately, Judah got very sick on this trip and died.

Nevertheless, Judah's dream lived on, and in time, the railroad he had envisioned was built. The Central Pacific Railroad became a reality, and the Big Four became fabulously wealthy.

RACE ACROSS THE WEST

Students read about the two railroad companies, the Central Pacific Railroad and the Union Pacific. They learn how they competed to finish the most tracks to build the transcontinental railroad.

Each student will then create a pop-up book featuring a section of railroad track crossing through some American scenery.

MATERIALS

- pages 91 and 92, reproduced for each student
- 12" x 18" (30.5 x 45.5 cm) white construction paper
- gray and black construction paper scraps
- colored pencils
- scissors
- glue
- reference books on the states

STEPS TO FOLLOW

1. Read and discuss the information about railroads from page 91.

2. Each student is assigned (or chooses) a state to research briefly. Students identify the natural environment that defines or typifies their state. Examples such as a mountain range in the Rockies, a desert in the Southwest, or prairie grasses for the Midwest are suggested.

3. To make the pop-up, have students fold the construction paper in half.

4. Direct students to cut and fold two tabs as shown.

5. Instruct students to open the folded construction paper and pull the tabs to the inside, reversing the fold.

6. Then have students cut out strips of black construction paper to form the ties of a railroad track. Have them cut out two narrow strips of gray construction paper to form the rails. Glue these pieces at the base of the tabs to form the railroad track.

7. Direct students to color, cut out, and then glue the locomotive engine to the tabs.

8. Instruct students make a landscape scene of their state on the top half of the folded construction paper. Students may choose to cut out shapes from construction paper to glue to their picture.

9. Have students cut out and then staple the information about the railroads from page 91 below the railroad tracks.

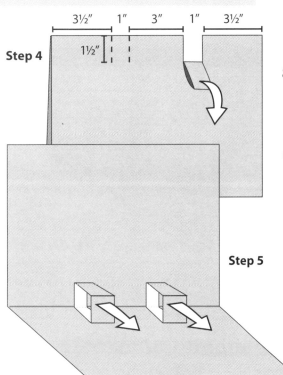

Step 4

3½"   1"   3"   1"   3½"

1½"

Step 5

RACE ACROSS THE WEST

RACE ACROSS THE WEST

While the Central Pacific Railroad was beginning to lay tracks from the West, another railroad company was formed in the East. This was the Union Pacific Railroad Company. Both companies convinced the government to give them land on which to build and lots of money. The two companies were to work as fast as possible, one from the East and the other from the West. They were to meet somewhere near the center of the country. The race was on.

The Central Pacific Railroad started in California and went east. It had the hardest challenge. It had to find a way to cross the rugged mountains. This meant blasting tunnels through solid rock. It meant carving ledges along sheer cliffs. It meant building towering trestles to cross deep ravines. The job seemed almost impossible, but the work went slowly on.

The Union Pacific Railroad started in Nebraska and went west. The crews for the Union Pacific did not have mountains to contend with, but they did have hills, rivers, and deserts to cross. In the winter, they had to work in blizzard conditions, digging through piles of drifted snow in freezing weather. It was difficult work for all involved.

Both companies wanted to lay as much track as possible. The government was paying lots of money for the work. The more miles of track laid, the more money the company would make. The companies began to push their crews to work faster and faster. They did not care if the work was done well. Tracks were laid over snow and ice, which would melt and cause the tracks to buckle. Bridges were built quickly and without care. In many places, the tracks were flimsy and dangerous. Later, many miles of track would have to be completely rebuilt! However, the companies did not care. They rushed ahead.

Finally, on May 10, 1869, the two railroads were joined at Promontory Summit near Ogden, Utah. At last, railroad tracks stretched all the way across the country, uniting the country in a new way.

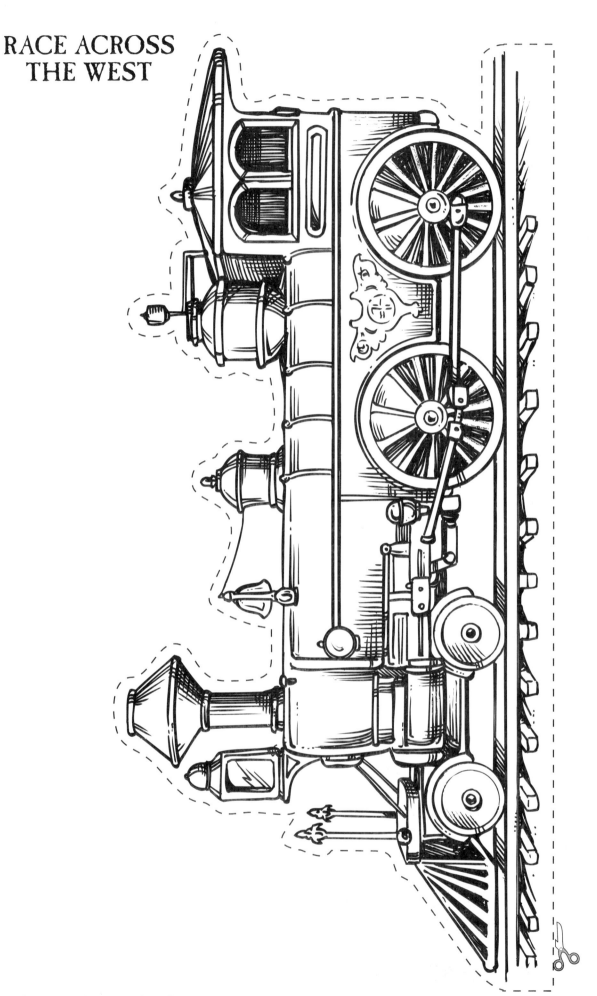

CHANGING THE FACE OF THE NATION

The Chinese Laborers

When the Big Four set out to build their railroad, they found that it was difficult to hire workers. Irish immigrants were willing to do the hard labor, but there were not nearly enough of them available. The Chinese immigrants who had come to work in the gold and silver mines offered their services.

The Chinese laborers proved that they could indeed keep up. They also showed that they were good engineers, solving difficult construction problems. Once, the Central Pacific Railroad seemed to be at a standstill. The tracks had come to a halt right at the base of a steep rock cliff. The Chinese laborers wove buckets out of tough reeds. Then they climbed into the buckets and were hauled up the face of the cliff. They chipped away at the rock until there was a ledge large enough to stand on. Then they worked from this ledge, hammering and blasting away at the rock. In time, they created a roadway large enough for the railroad bed.

In addition to their valuable skills, the Chinese laborers were much less troublesome than many of the other workers. They did not get drunk or fight amongst themselves. They were quiet, clean, and polite. Soon, the Big Four were importing workers directly from China.

Chinese immigrants came by the shiploads to work on the railroads. Life in their own country was difficult since they could not find work. The chance to work on the railroad, as tough as it was, seemed like an opportunity to these men. Many of them hoped to make some money and then return to China. Some of them did achieve this goal. Others stayed to make a new life in America. Many Chinese laborers died while constructing the railroad. It was very dangerous and difficult work, and thousands of workers of all nationalities were killed in various kinds of accidents.

The Chinese laborers contributed greatly to the building of the railroads. The railroads changed America and made it truly one nation from "sea to shining sea." The Chinese immigrants helped to build the America we live in today.

Name: _____

CHANGING THE FACE OF THE NATION

The completion of the railroads brought great changes to the United States. The nation had survived a bloody war that united the North and the South. The iron rails united the country from east to west. A traveler heading from New York to California could make the journey in 8 to 10 days, instead of several grueling months! Goods could be quickly shipped from place to place.

How do you think the railroads might have changed the lives of the following people? Write your answers in complete sentences.

A California settler who had gone west during the Gold Rush:

_____

_____

A Chinese immigrant who had come to work on building the railroad:

_____

_____

A Plains Indian:

_____

_____

The owner of a shoe factory in New York:

_____

_____

A man who made his living organizing and leading groups of wagons to California:

_____

_____

EMC 3704 • *Moving West* • ©2003 by Evan-Moor Corp.

MOVING WEST—REFLECTION SHEET

Name: _____ Date: _____

Directions: Please fill out this sheet after you have completed *History Pockets—Moving West.* Place your reflection sheet in Pocket 1.

1. When I look through my Moving West book, I feel _____

   because _____

   _____

   _____

2. The project I liked doing the most was the _____

   because _____

   _____

   _____

3. The project I liked doing the least was the _____

   because _____

   _____

   _____

4. Three things I am most proud of in my Moving West book are _____

   _____

   _____

   _____

5. Three things I would do differently to improve my Moving West book are _____

   _____

   _____

   _____

6. Three facts that I learned about the westward movement that I did not know before doing this

   project are_____

   _____

   _____

MOVING WEST—EVALUATION SHEET

Directions: Look through all the pockets and evaluate how well the activities were completed. Use the following point system:

6 outstanding	**5** excellent	**4** very good	**3** satisfactory	**2** some effort	**1** little effort	**0** no effort

Self-Evaluation	**Peer Evaluation**	**Teacher Evaluation**
Name: _____	Name: _____	____ completed assignments
____ completed assignments	____ completed assignments	____ followed directions
____ followed directions	____ followed directions	____ had correct information
____ had correct information	____ had correct information	____ edited writing
____ edited writing	____ edited writing	____ showed creativity
____ showed creativity	____ showed creativity	____ displayed neatness
____ displayed neatness	____ displayed neatness	____ added color
____ added color	____ added color	____ **total points**
____ **total points**	____ **total points**	____ **grade**
Comments: _____	Comments: _____	Comments: _____

EMC 3704 • Moving West • ©2003 by Evan-Moor Corp.